Developing Skills
WRITING

for KS3 tests

Andrew Bennett • Brian Conroy
Michele Paule • Alice Washbourne

Heinemann

Inspiring generations

Heinemann Educational Publishers
Halley Court, Jordan Hill, Oxford OX2 8EJ
Part of Harcourt Education

Heinemann is the registered trademark of
Harcourt Education Limited

© Andrew Bennett, Brian Conroy, Michele Paule, Alice Washbourne, 2003

First published 2004

07 06 05
10 9 8 7 6 5 4 3

British Library Cataloguing in Publication Data is available
from the British Library on request.

ISBN 0 435 10737 2

Designed by Hicksdesign
Produced by Bridge Creative Services Limited, Bicester, Oxon
Original illustrations © Harcourt Education Limited, 2003
Illustrated by Phil Healey: page 12, 56, 111, Catherine Howes: page 15, Kathryn Baker:
page 16, Chris Brown: page 19, 100, 107, Chris Molan: page 28, Chris Rothero: page 31,
Andrew Morris: page 34, 41, 60, 150, Mark Draisey: page 36, 50, 56, 68, 74, 152,
Melanie Sharp: page 70, 71, 97, Paul McCaffrey: page 89, 93, Kath Walker: page 92,
151, Pantelis Palios: page 120, 148, 153.

Cover design by GD Associates

Printed and bound in Italy by Printer Trento S.r.l.

Contents

Introduction

Developing Skills in Writing has been designed to help you develop your writing skills for the writing tests at the end of Year 9. It will build on your strengths and help you identify areas that you need to improve.

This book contains stimulating ideas for writing to help you understand how to create the different types of text that writers use every day. There is a wide range of challenging writing activities and plenty of help to support and guide you with the craft of writing. The book also shows you how to produce written responses that will help you to get maximum marks in the test.

Developing Skills in Writing is divided into six sections:

Sections A–D give you the opportunity to explore the four writing triplets creatively. These triplets reflect the different types of writing you find in everyday life and use in other school subjects. They are:

Section A	Imagine, explore, entertain
Section B	Inform, explain, describe
Section C	Persuade, argue, advise
Section D	Analyse, review, comment

In these sections you will revise the conventions of these text types and learn how they work by exploring fiction and non-fiction texts by a range of different writers. The writing activities in each section have been carefully selected to enable you to approach different kinds of written tasks imaginatively and independently.

Section E contains information about the KS3 writing tests and guidance on how to write the best answers to the questions. There are also practice tests so that you can become more familiar with the kinds of writing tasks that you will meet in the actual tests.

Section F provides a bank of key writing skills that you will need for the writing tasks in Sections A–D. You can use this section to help you practise word and sentence level writing skills.

Developing Skills in Writing will help you to do well in your tests and will also provide a solid foundation for the future. More importantly, it will help you to become a more skilful and confident writer – and that will help you in all areas of the school curriculum.

We hope you enjoy using this book and wish you every success as a writer.

Andrew Bennett
Brian Conroy
Michele Paule
Alice Washbourne

A Writing to imagine, explore, entertain

Writers may help readers use their imagination with a fantasy novel; they could explore teenage issues in a TV series; they might entertain readers with a gossip piece on a pop star. Writers use many different forms of writing to help readers use their imagination, explore ideas or simply to entertain them. In this section, you will explore a range of fiction and non-fiction texts and use the skills that you learn to create your own pieces of writing.

Unit A1 will help you to capture your readers' imagination by creating settings, characters and atmosphere, and with your choice of detail, imaginative vocabulary, similes and metaphors. You will also learn how to vary sentences and structure paragraphs effectively.
Unit A2 will help you to explore ideas, things and places in your writing by using language and structure to achieve particular effects. You will also look at the ways in which you can link whole pieces of writing effectively to appeal to your readers.
Unit A3 will help you to convey ideas, create expectations and use humour in your writing to entertain your readers by varying the structure, pace and language. You will also look at the effects of repetition and contrast, formality and informality, and try out these techniques for yourself.

Think about what you already know about writing to imagine, explore and entertain. Using a brainstorm diagram like the one below, explore the different forms of writing you would expect to find and their features. Add notes to explain how they would help you to imagine, explore and entertain. Some examples have been done for you.

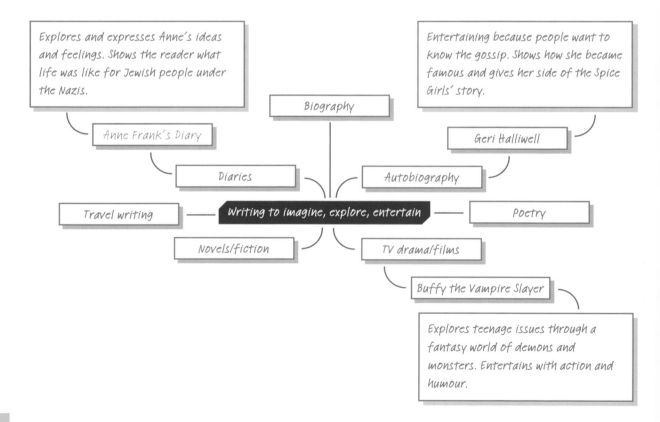

Explores and expresses Anne's ideas and feelings. Shows the reader what life was like for Jewish people under the Nazis.

Entertaining because people want to know the gossip. Shows how she became famous and gives her side of the Spice Girls' story.

Biography

Anne Frank's Diary

Geri Halliwell

Diaries

Autobiography

Travel writing — Writing to imagine, explore, entertain — Poetry

Novels/fiction

TV drama/films

Buffy the Vampire Slayer

Explores teenage issues through a fantasy world of demons and monsters. Entertains with action and humour.

A1 Imagine

When you imagine something, you can let your mind run free to create a make-believe situation. Writing an imaginative piece involves expressing your ideas in ways that will help your readers to imagine too. In this unit you will write the opening chapter of a story.

You will focus on:

- creating the setting and atmosphere
- creating the characters
- making an impact with the structure of your story.

↘ Setting and atmosphere

TRP
p5

When you write a story, it is important to create a vivid setting and atmosphere to keep your readers' interest. You will learn to write a paragraph using your imagination and different techniques to build up a vivid impression of the setting.

Setting

The setting is the place and time in which the action is set. It is an important part of creating the right mood. Writers need to create a strong sense of place to help readers imagine that they are there. To do this, writers need to:

- choose the setting carefully, including the place, season, time of day, etc.
- choose the details well to build up a strong image in the readers' minds.

ACTIVITY 1

1 Look at the brainstorm diagram below. It shows some ideas for the setting of a story about bullying at school.

2 Create your own brainstorm to help you to generate ideas for a setting for a story about a teenage runaway.

> Season: winter – grey skies, cold wind, possibly rain

> Sounds: bell goes off, laughter of pupils, thundering footsteps as everyone rushes to get home, teachers calling out for quiet

> Time of day: end of school – late afternoon, getting darker

> **Setting for a story about bullying at school**

> Place: school corridor – peeling paint, graffiti, dirty windows, torn displays on the walls

> Smells: waft of cold school dinners, dust and chalk, chemicals from science lab

Choosing and using details to create atmosphere

In the extract below, a man is sitting in a park and thinking of a time when he sat there before. P.D. James is famous for the atmosphere she creates in her novels.

ACTIVITY 2

Read the extract carefully.

a   Find the details listed in the chart below.

b   Explore the effects the writer has created by using them in the next activity and complete a similar chart with your ideas.

> Staring at the lake through the boughs of a willow, he realised that he had sat in this identical spot eight months previously, in his lunch hour the day after his wife's death. It had been an unusually cold Friday in November ... In these burgeoning rose beds there had been a few tight red buds, blighted by the cold, their stems choked with dead leaves. The lake had been bronzed and wrinkled with, at its centre, a great salver of beaten silver. An old man, surely too old to be employed by the city council, had shuffled along the path past him, spearing the sparse litter. The park then had held an air of sad decrepitude, the handrail of the blue bridge worn by tourists' hands, the fountain silent, and the tea house closed for the winter. Now the air was loud with the staccato chatter of tourists, the shrieks and laughter of children. Then, he remembered, there had been one solitary child with his mother. The gulls had risen squawking before his harsh, cracked laughter, and he had stretched out his arms, willing their plump bodies to fall into his palms. Under the far trees patches of early snow had lain between the clumps of grass like the discarded litter of the dead summer.

> From *Innocent Blood* by P.D. James

Detail	Effect
a few tight red buds, blighted by the cold, their stems choked with dead leaves.	Describing dying flowers creates a depressing mood, especially through words like `blighted` and `choked`.
The lake had been bronzed and wrinkled with, at its centre, a great salver of beaten silver.	Dull grey colours add to the mood.
the fountain silent, and the tea house closed for the winter.	
Now the air was loud with the staccato chatter of tourists, the shrieks and laughter of children.	The contrast between now and then makes the past seem sadder.
before his harsh, cracked laughter,	
early snow had lain between the clumps of grass like the discarded litter of the dead summer.	

ACTIVITY 3

Now create your own setting for a story about a teenage runaway. Use some of the techniques that you explored in the extract on page 8. In your writing, you will create:

- mood through the details you describe
- contrast to make the mood stronger.

First, plan the setting for your story. Use the planning grid below to generate ideas. Some examples have been given to get you started, but you do not have to use them in your story.

	Detail	Why I have chosen it
Place	A shop doorway in a back street.	It is a lonely and depressing setting where my character would not feel safe.
Season		
Time of day		
Weather		
Sounds		
Sights/colours		
Smells		
Touch	Hardness of the step; coldness of the air.	To help readers imagine the uncomfortable situation.
Other people and what they do		
Contrast	Memories of warm bedroom and mum's cooking.	To create a contrast with the runaway's hunger and cold now.

TIMED WRITING *(15 minutes)*

Use your ideas for the teenage runaway story from your planning grid to draft the opening paragraph. Create atmosphere by building up a vivid description of the setting.

Creating characters

When you create a character in a story, you need to think about how you are going to give readers a vivid impression of that person through the details you describe and the words you choose. The golden rule is **show, don't tell**. This means that it is better to build up an image or idea in the readers' minds than to make statements about the character.
In the extract below, the writer describes Mildred, the carer who looks after the grandmother of the teenage narrator, Bridget.

Mildred has a thing about belts. She has three coats, a tweed one, a cloth one and a raincoat and they all have belts which Mildred straps viciously round her fat middle. They must be so uncomfortable but then comfort never seems to be high on Mildred's list of priorities. She makes no concessions to it. She wears her grey hair in a bun which is not only secured by a fierce looking elastic band but is further anchored with incredibly long, wide steel hairgrips. Mildred reminds me of a jeep, all squat and solid, all weight and rigid lines. She used to be a bus conductress and though she retired long before they came into use she sees Pay-as-you-enter buses, with drivers only, as the true indication of the decline of our civilisation. She treats Grandma exactly like a passenger on a bus and I'm quite surprised she doesn't give her a ticket when she leaves. Right now, she's unbuckling her belt and taking her hat off and her coat off and bustling about claiming her territory. Eventually, she plonks her short, stout body down on the chair just vacated by Bridget and asks Grandma how she is today.

> From *Have the Men Had Enough?* by Margaret Forster

It's all in the detail

The writer has created an impression, which could be summarised like this:

Mildred is a big woman who dresses badly. She always belts her coats and wears her hair up. She is old-fashioned in some of her views. She likes to be in control and she doesn't really care about Grandma.

Why do you think the writer chose to create such a detailed picture instead of just giving us the facts? What is the effect on readers?

ACTIVITY 4

1 a Read the extract above and think about what each highlighted detail adds to your impression of Mildred.
  b Make a chart like the one below, adding your own comments about each of the highlighted details as shown.

Detail	What it suggests about Mildred
'she sees Pay-as-you-enter buses, with drivers only, as the true indication of the decline of our civilisation.'	Suggests she is used to complaining about the modern world and sees modern conveniences as a bad thing.

2 Now create another similar chart for a character you are going to invent to include in your story about the teenage runaway.

   a Choose one of the characters below or invent your own:

- a shy new Year 7 pupil
- a nosy neighbour
- a busy parent
- a kind grandparent.
- a school bully

   b Decide on the sort of detail you would include to build a vivid impression and fill this in on your chart.

Using similes and metaphors

The writer of the extract on page 10 tells us:

'Mildred reminds me of a jeep, all squat and solid, all weight and rigid lines.'

The writer gives a clearer impression of what Mildred is like by comparing her with something else. If she had wanted to create a very different sort of character, she might have written:

> She reminds me of a swan, all elegance and grace and flowing lines.

ACTIVITY 5

What might the following similes and metaphors suggest about the characters involved?

a He was a volcano of a man, who would erupt at any small annoyance.

b Her eyes were like dirty puddles on a motorway, her hair like old grass trimmings, and her coat looked like the dried hide of a long-dead animal.

c Jake's scared rabbit eyes peeped out from behind the door.

 REMEMBER

→ In a **simile** the writer compares one thing with another using 'as' or 'like', for example 'He looked like an enormous jelly baby'.

→ In a **metaphor**, the writer describes something as if it were actually something else, for example 'The moon is a balloon'. The words 'as' and 'like' are not used.

 TIMED WRITING *(10 minutes)*

TRP
p5

Brainstorm some similes and metaphors to build a clearer description of the character you chose in Activity 4.

Using verbs, adverbs and adverbial phrases

When the writer describes Mildred's actions, she does so using effective verbs, adverbs and adverbial phrases. For example, when she writes about Mildred's belts, she doesn't just write 'Mildred does her belts up', she writes: '... belts which Mildred straps viciously round her fat middle'. This description is more effective because:

● the verb 'straps' suggests discipline – is she trying to train her stomach?

● the adverb 'viciously' suggests the violence of her action

● 'straps viciously round her fat middle' – combined together, this phrase suggests she hates her body and is punishing it.

ACTIVITY 6

1 Compare the sentences below. Which one creates the strongest impression? Why?

  ● My sister Anya walked in.

  ● My sister Anya walked in angrily.

  ● Slamming the door so hard it shook the frame, my sister Anya stomped in.

2 Using the character you created in Activity 4 on page 11, write one or two sentences that describe them entering a room in an appropriate way. That might be:

  ● nervously   ● confidently   ● secretively

  ● in a rush   ● shyly   ● absent-mindedly.

For example:

> Jason shyly peered round the door of the science lab before he crept nervously to a seat at the back.

 TIMED WRITING *(15 minutes)*

Write a paragraph describing a character who might appear in your story about the teenage runaway.

 REMEMBER

To create a vivid interesting character, choose the following carefully:

→ details

→ similes and metaphors

→ verbs, adverbs and adverbial phrases.

Creating impact through structure

You have looked at the ways in which writers can choose and use details and words to create vivid descriptions for their readers. The structure of your writing – from the plot to the construction of paragraphs, sentences and clauses – is also part of the craft of good writing.

ACTIVITY 7

1 Think of a story or film that you know well. Where would you expect to find:
   a the introduction of the main characters
   b a marriage
   c who committed a crime
   d the key moment that everything else depends on
   e a big argument or separation between two lovers?

   Can you think of some examples from stories or films that you know? For example in the film 'Sixth Sense' we are introduced to the main characters at the start; the Doctor realises the little boy really does see ghosts and decides to help him in the middle; the twist where we realise that the doctor himself is a ghost comes at the end. The Harry Potter books usually start with a description of Harry at home with the Dursleys, then he escapes to Hogwarts where he faces a big problem with his friends, which they overcome against huge odds; he usually stars in a Quidditch game along the way, too.

2 What would be the effect if the order of events (the structure of the plot) in the story or film you thought of was changed?

Opening sentences for maximum effect

Read the following sentences. Each one is taken from the beginning of a novel. How has the writer caught the reader's interest in each case?

> The last minutes of the last lesson of the last day of term were ticking away, and Martin Turner could not wait to be set free.

> From *Face* by Benjamin Zephaniah

> It was the day my grandmother exploded.

> From *The Crow Road* by Iain Banks

> Lyra and her daemon moved through the darkening Hall, taking care to keep to one side, out of sight of the kitchen.

> From *Northern Lights* by Philip Pullman

ACTIVITY 8

Write three different openings for your story about the teenage runaway. Make sure the sentences:

- grab the readers' attention
- give some clues about the story's subject.

Structuring paragraphs

You can make your paragraphs interesting for readers in a range of ways: You can:
- build suspense or drop clues and hints along the way.
- open them dramatically
- save important information until the end

ACTIVITY 9

1   Read the paragraphs below from the opening of *Northern Lights*. Comment on the highlighted parts and their effects on readers – one has been done for you as an example.

> Lyra and her daemon moved through the darkening Hall, taking care to keep to one side, out of sight of the kitchen. The three great tables that ran the length of the Hall were laid already, the silver and the glass catching what little light there was, and the long benches were pulled out ready for the guests. Portraits of former Masters hung high up in the gloom along the walls. Lyra reached the dais and looked back at the open kitchen door, and, seeing no one, stepped up beside the high table. The places here were laid with gold, not silver, and the fourteen seats were not oak benches but mahogany chairs with velvet cushions.
>
> Lyra stopped beside the Master's chair and flicked the biggest glass gently with a fingernail. The sound rang clearly through the Hall.

Suggests a grand place and a special occasion – I wonder where and what.

> From *Northern Lights* by Philip Pullman

2   Now think about the structure of these paragraphs. How has the structure helped to achieve the impact? Consider:
- how and why the writer has created a gloomy atmosphere
- how he has made it seem frightening and intimidating
- how the sense that Lyra should not be there is achieved
- what idea we get of Lyra
- why the writer has Lyra flick the glass after he has built up these impressions.

Shaping sentences for maximum effect

The way sentences are structured – their length and the order of the clauses – can be just as important as the words in them. Sentence structure can make the difference between an interesting and a boring piece of writing.

ACTIVITY 10

1   Recreate each of the sentences below to convey the maximum impact and most vivid effect for your readers. You can change some of the words as well as the structures if you can think of better ones.
   a   She sat up. She looked around the room. It was empty. She was scared. She wondered where they had all gone.
   b   The bell rang. Jack ran for the classroom door. His shirt was hanging out. He knocked his books to the floor. He opened the door.
   c   I looked at the exam paper. The question was too hard. I didn't know what to do.
   d   My grandpa snored. His moustache moved. His paper was open on his stomach. The pages moved up and down.

2   Then explain the changes you have made and why. The first has been done for you as an example.

> a   Trembling, she sat up and looked around her at the empty room. Where had everybody gone?
>
> I started with 'trembling' and got rid of 'she was scared' because I wanted to show her fear straight away and suggest that she is shaking all through the action. I turned the first three sentences into one sentence – this creates more suspense. I turned the last sentence into a rhetorical question to suggest her thoughts, make it more vivid and add impact at the end.

TIMED WRITING *(30 minutes)*

Write the opening chapter of the story about the teenage runaway.
Use structuring features carefully to build on the writing you have already done.
Look back at the planning chart you created in Activity 4 on page 11 and use the
same technique to create any other characters you want to introduce.

 REMEMBER

Make sure that you:
→ choose and use details carefully to build up the setting and atmosphere
→ create vivid characters with your choice of similes and metaphors
→ use effective verbs, adverbs and adverbial phrases to create interesting sentences
→ vary the length of the sentences
→ structure your paragraphs to build interest.

A2 Explore

When you explore ideas, people, things and places in your writing, you need to balance information with your own personal response. In this unit, you will look at examples of travel writing and you will write a travel piece.

You will focus on:
- creating opening sentences
- using a variety of paragraph openings
- balancing information with personal response
- structuring and linking paragraphs effectively.

↘ Opening sentences

ACTIVITY 1

1   Create a brainstorm diagram like the one below showing more reasons why an opening sentence is important.

> To get the readers' attention and make them want to read on

Opening sentences

> To be dramatic or surprising

2   The sentences below are all opening sentences from travel writing. For each one, decide:
   a   what techniques you think the writer is using
   b   why you think that the writer decided to begin this way.
   The first one has been done for you as an example:

> The opening words create a sense of distance, as though it might be a long time ago. This makes it mysterious.

> 'night-time journey' tells us what he is writing about and adds a sense of romance.

a   I do not recall how much my memories of that night-time journey were the creation of fitful dreams or the stuff of actuality.

> The contrast of dreams and reality suggests it might be a strange story and helps gain our interest.

> From *Triple Alliance* by Philip Clarke

b Where's the army?

> From *Questions in El Salvador* by David Brierly

c During the night the rats stole my soap.

> From *Five Days in Guinea* by Andrew Dinwoodie

d The night is pitch black, the jungle sparkles with fireflies.

> From *Boys' Own Expedition* by Nick Kirke

e Depression lurked over me like a Lakeland storm-sky: oppressive, inevitable and apparently unending.

> From *Midnight on Mont Blanc* by R.G. Willis

3 Now try creating a different opening sentence for a piece of writing about a school trip. Here are some examples.
I knew straight away that I was wearing the wrong shoes.
The coach had arrived but where were my mates?
The rain is pouring down and the road stretches ahead, wet and shiny.
It is hard to know whether my fears about the Year 8 camping trip were the result of my big brother's horror stories or my own natural nervousness.

You could use the following ideas to help you:

● the excitement of the night before

● setting off

● arriving

● a moment of disaster.

↘ Opening paragraphs

TRP
p6

ACTIVITY 2

Read the extracts below and on page 20. They follow on from three of the sentences you read in Activity 1 on page 18 and form the opening paragraphs of those texts.

a   Decide how each of the paragraphs:

- sustains the readers' interest
- gives an idea of what the rest of the text will be
- sets the style and/or tone.

b   What techniques do the writers use to achieve these effects? Use the checklist below to help you.

- Past or present tense? Why?
- Similes and/or metaphors.
- Direct speech for immediacy and interest.
- Rhetorical questions to make readers think.

- Repetition for effect.
- Humour.
- Choice of detail.
- Contrast.

Depression lurked over me like a Lakeland storm-sky: oppressive, inevitable and apparently unending. 'What you need', said Bernie over the top of his beer, 'is to take your mind off it; get out onto the hill. Let's go and climb Mont Blanc. We can drive down on your bike.'

> From *Midnight on Mont Blanc* by R.G. Willis

Where's the army? Why aren't they guarding the airport? At Belize, a twenty-minute hop away, there are camouflage nets and sandbags and RAF Hawks and squaddies with pink British faces. At El Salvador International Airport, not a single soldier, in a country torn by civil war.

> From *Questions in El Salvador* by David Brierly

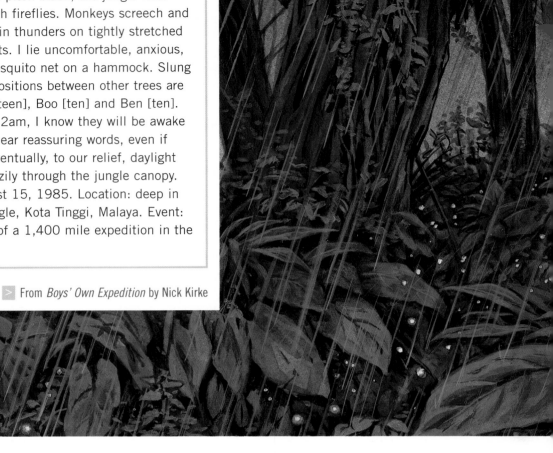

The night is pitch black, the jungle floor sparkles with fireflies. Monkeys screech and monsoon rain thunders on tightly stretched groundsheets. I lie uncomfortable, anxious, within a mosquito net on a hammock. Slung in similar positions between other trees are Alexis [fourteen], Boo [ten] and Ben [ten]. Though it's 2am, I know they will be awake and won't hear reassuring words, even if shouted. Eventually, to our relief, daylight emerges hazily through the jungle canopy. Date: August 15, 1985. Location: deep in primary jungle, Kota Tinggi, Malaya. Event: the climax of a 1,400 mile expedition in the Far East.

> From *Boys' Own Expedition* by Nick Kirke

TIMED WRITING *(15 minutes)*

Using the opening sentence you wrote about a school trip for Activity 1 on page 18, develop your idea into an opening paragraph. Use some of the techniques used by the writers in the extracts on pages 19 and 20.

↘ Balance of information and personal response

Travel writing can be as much about exploring people's reactions to places, as it is about the places themselves. Travel writers often explore the ideas and feelings they have, as well as describe their surroundings. Good travel writing often:

- achieves a balance of information and personal writing
- uses a range of techniques to convey a vivid sense of place and emotion to keep the readers' interest
- structures writing skilfully to link the different parts
- makes links to help readers imagine things they have not experienced.

ACTIVITY 3

The extract below is by Sarah Wheeler, a writer who spent months in the Antarctic in 1999, where she was able to visit the hut of her hero, the famous Captain Scott, whose exploration party died trying to get back from the South Pole in 1912.

1 As you read the text, make a note of:
   a which parts of the text give you information
   b which parts of the text tell you about the writer's feelings and reactions.

The ice was more than four feet thick wherever we drilled it, and an hour after we set out for Cape Evans, around Big Razorback island, we lay down among the Weddell seals.

'Listen to that', said Ann. It was a faint scraping sound, like hard cheese on a grater.

'The pups are weaned', she announced. 'It's their teeth raking against the edge of the ice holes.'

Adult Weddells weigh up to 1000 pounds and are able to live further south than any other seals because they can maintain an open hole in the ice with their teeth. Ann went off to photograph them doing it, and I pressed my ear to the ice and heard the adults underneath calling their ancient song, **ululant** and **ineffably** sad.

Later, I recognised the gabled ridged roof and weatherboard cladding of the hut in the distance. It was a prefabricated hut, made in England and shipped south in pieces... When I pushed open the wooden door I smelt my grandmother's house when I was a child – coal dust and burnt coal – and it was chilly, as it used to be at six o'clock in the morning when I followed my grandfather downstairs to scrape out the grate ... It was the familiarity of the surroundings which struck my English sensibility – the blue-and-orange Huntley and Palmer biscuit boxes, green-and-gold tins of Lyle's golden syrup, ... and the shape of the label on Heinz tomato ketchup bottles ... I still lived with many of these products and ... they ... intensified the hut experience ...

A single beam of sunlight fell on the bunk in Scott's quarters ...

> From *Terra Incognita* by Sarah Wheeler

Word bank
ululant: sounding grief-stricken **ineffably:** too extreme to explain

2 Now think about the way the writer has organised her writing.

  a Decide whether each paragraph:

- describes feelings and/or reactions.

- narrates events
- gives information

  b Decide why you think the writer has included each of the seven paragraphs. Complete a chart like the one below, using your own ideas. Some examples have been given to get you started.

Paragraph	What it does	Why I think it is there
1	Narrates events – tells us what they are doing.	As an introduction – to move the writing on from what went before.
2 & 3	Direct speech and action are described – gives some information about the seals.	Makes the writing more lively and immediate.

TIMED WRITING *(15 minutes)*

1 Imagine you have been asked to write a travel piece about a school trip. Plan:

  a how you will introduce it

  b what information you might include to interest your readers

  c what feelings and/or reactions you will include to create a vivid picture of your experience.

Complete a planning grid like the one below. Some ideas have been included to start you off.

Introduction	● *arriving at the school gates with a suitcase*
Information to include	*journey – holiday centre –dormitory – canoe trip*
Reactions / feelings	*excited – looking forward to the trip – homesick, missing my dog – terrified of being in the canoe*

2 Now think about how you will structure your ideas in your travel piece.

REMEMBER

When you are planning the structure of a piece of writing:

→ description can be used to set the scene at the beginning

→ speech and passages can be used to make your writing more lively and immediate

→ information passages can give readers important information, but be careful that they are not too long or boring

→ description of your responses or feelings helps readers to imagine they are seeing through your eyes and sharing the experience; it can also be used to reflect on the experience and is a good way to finish your piece of writing.

↳ Joined-up thinking

The writer of the extract in Activity 3 also manages to keep the readers' interest by using different ways to open paragraphs and by linking parts of the text to give it continuity.

ACTIVITY 4

1   Find these paragraph openings in the extract on page 21:
    ● 'Listen to that', said Ann.'
    ● 'Adult Weddells weigh up to 1000 pounds and are able to live further south than any other seals because they can maintain an open hole in the ice with their teeth.'
    ● 'Later, I recognised the gabled ridged roof and weatherboard cladding of the hut in the distance.'
    ● 'A single beam of sunlight fell on the bunk in Scott's quarters …'

2   How does each opening achieve one or more of the following:
    ● capture the readers' interest
    ● indicate the contents and/or subject of the paragraph?
    ● help order events

3   Using the planning grid for your piece of writing about a school trip that you completed for the timed writing assignment on page 22, decide on the order in which you will present the paragraphs. For example, decide whether you will group all the information together or alternate between information and personal response.

4   Choose one of the paragraphs and write a first draft of it. Remember to:
    ● choose the paragraph opening for interest and to indicate content/tone
    ● make sure the order of events is clear.

REMEMBER

There are useful words to help you order the things you want to say, for example:
● at first   ● initially   ● next   ● later
● finally   ● in the end   ● at last.

→   Information is often presented in the passive. For example:

> *The holiday centre was <u>opened in</u> …*

→   Beginning a paragraph sentence with a verb or adverb can create a vivid impression. For example:

> *<u>Trying</u> to disguise my nerves, I …*   *<u>Slowly</u>, I got out of my dad's car …*

⅃ Tricks of the trade

Now you will focus on some of the key techniques and 'tricks of the trade' that writers use to keep their readers interested.

The power of three

Three can be a magic number in writing. The repetition of words or clause structures in threes is a technique frequently used by the writers of speeches and advertisements. This is because they know this technique can:

- add rhythm to sentences
- help to give a powerful impact through repetition
- help to build up to a climax.

Read the following extracts and think about how each writer has used the power of three.

> DOOLITTLE [most musical, most melancholy] I'll tell you, Governor, if you'll only let me get a word in. I'm willing to tell you. I'm wanting to tell you. I'm waiting to tell you.
> HIGGINS. Pickering: this chap has a certain natural gift of rhetoric. Observe the rhythm of his native woodnotes wild. 'I'm willing to tell you: I'm wanting to tell you: I'm waiting to tell you.' Sentimental rhetoric! That's the Welsh strain in him. It also accounts for his mendacity and dishonesty.

> From *Pygmalion* by George Bernard Shaw

In Africa, as in the UK, there are some groups of people, such as women and disabled people, who are more disadvantaged than others. They find it harder than most to fulfil their potential, to access services to meet their basic needs, or to obtain their fundamental rights.
On Red Nose Day everyone in England, Scotland, Wales and Northern Ireland is encouraged to cast inhibitions aside, put on a red nose, and do something a little bit silly to raise money.

> From the Comic Relief website

They all sprang into action. First they had to clear the table, then they had to assign tasks: one collected the chickens, another drew water from the well, a third was in charge of wood from the stove. There would be no ironing, no embroidery, no sewing that day.

> From *Like Water for Chocolate* by Laura Esquival

ACTIVITY 5

Using the following situations, create sentences of your own using the power of three to achieve an impact on your readers. One sentence has been given for the first situation, but you might think of others.

a   Describe the boredom of a rainy Sunday afternoon.

> *There was no sun in the sky, no film on TV and no chance my Mum would lend me the money to go to the cinema.*

b   Create sympathy for abandoned kittens for a charity appeal.
c   Create a scary idea of a huge wrestler.
d   Describe someone getting closer and closer to you as you are hiding.

Lists

Writers can use listing as a technique for a variety of reasons. For informative texts, lists are an efficient way of conveying maximum information. For writing that is meant to interest and entertain readers, lists can serve other purposes. For example, they can:

- build up a detailed picture
- create a sense of busyness and confusion
- create a sense of pace or routine.

ACTIVITY 6

1   Look at the examples below and decide what effect the writer is aiming for by using a listing technique.

> Before my mother came to visit I hoovered the stairs, washed the floors, cleaned the windows, dusted the shelves, books and vases, polished the tables, did the dishes and ironed the cushion covers. Of course, the first thing she said was 'I see you haven't cleaned your bathroom tiles'.

> Her dressing table was like a graveyard for dead make-up: half-squeezed tubes of foundation; dried-up mascara wands; smudged pots of eyeshadow; and run-down lipsticks.

> He gained the ball, bent it to the left, picked it up on the other side of the tackle, dribbled ten yards, brought it under control and neatly lifted it into the back of the net.

2   Use listing to create a description of one of the following:
- a classroom after the last class has left on a Friday
- a funfair or arcade
- a routine Sunday lunch or school dinner time
- your town centre on a Saturday afternoon.

REMEMBER

→   Use listing only when you want to create a particular effect.

→   Remember to punctuate lists properly – either with commas or semi-colons.

TIMED WRITING *(45 minutes)*

Write an article for the school magazine about a memorable school trip or outing. In your writing, make sure you:

● convey a vivid sense of the place and the experience

● interest your readers through your choice of language

● structure your writing to make it lively.

Copy and complete the planning grid below to help you plan your writing.

Ideas for the opening sentence(s):

Information:

Personal response:

Descriptive words and phrases:

Ideas for the ending:

Reminders for useful writing techniques:

 REMEMBER

Pay special attention to:

→ the opening

→ the structure of the paragraphs

→ using structuring in threes and listing.

→ the paragraph openings

→ your choice of detail

A3 Entertain

When you write to entertain, you are trying to do more than just make your readers laugh, although humour can be very effective. More broadly, entertaining writing keeps readers glued to the page and wanting to read more. In this unit, you will look at some of the techniques for achieving these effects and create your own piece of writing.

You will focus on:

- creating suspense
- using exaggeration to create humour, strong feelings and vivid pictures
- including exciting action.

ACTIVITY 1

1 Think of a book that you have read or a film or TV programme you have seen, which entertains in each of the ways listed above.
2 Note down your idea, and why and how it entertains in the way that it does.
3 Share your ideas with a partner or the rest of the class.

Some examples to get you started are given in the diagram.

> Harry Potter entertains you from the start with the humour and awfulness of the Dursley family and by the way the author creates sympathy for Harry.

> One of the ways The Simpsons entertains is through the unexpected — we expect parents to be responsible, so when Homer is lazy and selfish, it seems funny.

> In films, when someone is walking down a dark alley and the camera angle is from above so they look small, you are on the edge of your seat because you know they are going to be attacked.

Entertaining audiences

> Ghost stories entertain us when they are set in a spooky place that gives us the shivers. This also creates expectations — we know something is going to happen.

> The hospital drama ER entertains by having characters with problems the viewers get involved in and by being set in a dramatic emergency ward where there is always a life-or-death situation.

↘ Creating suspense

Writers can keep their readers hooked, determined to know what happens next, by using suspense. The secret to doing this effectively is to get readers to expect something and then to delay it. You can do this by:

- drawing out a description, so you get a good build-up
- creating distracting events so readers are kept waiting for the event they expect to happen.

ACTIVITY 2

Read the extract from *Jane Eyre* and work out how the writer has created suspense. Some annotations have been made to give you a start.

 REMEMBER

Writers can build suspense through:

→ their choice of detail and the way it is built up

→ varying the length of sentences to build up to a climax

→ the description of the character's responses and feelings

→ the way they delay the final moment.

In this extract, Jane, a young governess, lies in bed thinking about what could make her employer so reluctant to stay at his home, Thornfield, when she begins to hear strange things …

Jane Eyre

Though I had now extinguished my candle and was laid down in bed, I could not sleep for thinking of his look when he paused in the avenue, and told how his destiny had risen up before him, and dared him to be happy at Thornfield.

'Why not?' I asked myself. 'What alienates him from the house? Will he leave it again soon? Mrs Fairfax said he seldom stayed here longer than a fortnight at a time; and he has now been resident eight weeks. If he does go, the change will be doleful. Suppose he should be absent spring, summer, and autumn: how joyless sunshine and fine days will seem!'

I hardly know whether I had slept or not after this musing; at any rate, I started wide awake on hearing a vague murmur, peculiar and lugubrious, which sounded, I thought, just above me. I wished I had kept my candle burning: the night was drearily dark; my spirits were depressed. I rose and sat up in bed, listening. The sound was hushed.

> *Short sentences create tension.*

I tried again to sleep; but my heart beat anxiously: my inward tranquillity was broken. The clock, far down in the hall, struck two. Just then it seemed my chamber door was touched; as if fingers had swept the panels in groping a way along the dark gallery outside. I said, 'Who is there?' Nothing answered. I was chilled with fear.

All at once I remembered that it might be Pilot, who, when the kitchen-door chanced to be left open, not unfrequently found his way up to the threshold of Mr Rochester's chamber: I had seen him lying there myself in the mornings. The idea calmed me somewhat: I lay down. Silence composes the nerves; and as an unbroken hush now reigned again through the whole house, I began to feel the return of slumber. But it was not fated that I should sleep that night. A dream had scarcely approached my ear, when it fled affrighted, scared by a marrow-freezing incident enough.

> *Precise adjectives show the writer's mood.*

This was a demoniac laugh – low, suppressed, and deep – uttered, as it seemed, at the very keyhole of my chamber door. The head of my bed was near the door, and I thought at first the goblin-laughter stood at my bedside – or rather, crouched by my pillow: but I rose, looked round, and could see nothing; while, as I still gazed, the unnatural sound was reiterated: and I knew it came from behind the panels. My first impulse was to rise and fasten the bolt; my next, again to cry out, 'Who is there?'

Something gurgled and moaned.

> *Using the power of three to describe the strange laughter.*

> From *Jane Eyre* by Charlotte Brontë

ACTIVITY 3

Read the three scenarios below. Choose one and write two or three paragraphs full of suspense.

a You have borrowed your brother's or sister's favourite CD without permission. You are in his or her room, putting it back, when you see out of the window that he or she is returning. You have to put it back and get out of the room before you are discovered. In your rush, you knock something over.

b You are walking through a graveyard for a dare. You hear a noise and think someone is following you. You cannot see anything. You do not know the quickest way out.

c You are in the classroom. The teacher is going through the homework, asking questions. Everyone is scared of this teacher and you have been in trouble before for not having done your homework, even though it wasn't your fault. You are dreading the teacher asking you a question.

REMEMBER

You can create suspense through:
→ your choice of detail and the way you build it up
→ varying the length of sentences to build up to a climax
→ your description of the character's responses and feelings
→ the way you delay the final moment
→ making the final moment as dramatic or as unexpected as you can.

↘ Using exaggeration

If used carefully, exaggeration can be a useful tool for writers. However, the exaggeration must be carefully crafted to suit the purpose of the writing to be effective. Otherwise, the effect can sound ridiculous.

Exaggeration can be used to:

● gain the readers' attention
● build a vivid picture of a character or place
● suggest strong feelings such as terror or love from a character's point of view
● create a humorous effect.

Exaggeration can be achieved by:

● piling on the detail
● focusing on only one aspect, at great length
● using strong, dramatic language
● repeating the same idea in different ways
● repeating structures to create a strong effect
● repeating key words to create a strong effect.

ACTIVITY 4

Read the two extracts below and on page 32. Using the checklists about exaggeration, decide:

a   what effect each writer is trying to achieve through exaggeration; for example, humourous or dramatic

b   what techniques they are using.

The following extract describes the world of 18th-century Paris.

Perfume

In the period of which we speak, there reigned in the cities a stench barely conceivable to us modern men and women. The streets stank of manure, the courtyards of urine, the stairwells stank of mouldering wood and rat droppings, the kitchens of spoiled cabbage and mutton fat; the unaired parlours stank of stale dust, the bedrooms of greasy sheets, damp featherbeds, and the pungently sweet aroma of chamber pots. The stench of sulphur rose from the chimneys, the stench of caustic lyes from the tanneries, and from the slaughterhouses came the stench of congealed blood. People stank of sweat and unwashed clothes; from their mouths came the stench of rotting teeth, from their bellies that of onions and from their bodies, if they were no longer very young, came the stench of rancid cheese and sour milk and tumorous disease. The rivers stank, the marketplaces stank, the churches stank, it stank beneath the bridges and in the palaces. The peasant stank as did the priest, the apprentice did as did his master's wife, the whole of the aristocracy stank, even the King himself stank like a rank lion, and the Queen like an old goat, summer and winter. For in the eighteenth century there was nothing to hinder bacteria busy at decomposition, and so there was no human activity, either constructive or destructive, no manifestation of germinating or decaying life, that was not accompanied by stench.

> From *Perfume* by Patrick Süskind

In this extract a hard-headed Victorian businessman explains his ideas about education.

Hard Times

'NOW, what I want is, Facts. Teach these boys and girls nothing but Facts. Facts alone are wanted in life. Plant nothing else, and root out everything else. You can only form the minds of reasoning animals upon Facts: nothing else will ever be of any service to them. This is the principle on which I bring up my own children, and this is the principle on which I bring up these children. Stick to Facts, sir!'

The scene was a plain, bare, monotonous vault of a schoolroom, and the speaker's square forefinger emphasised his observations by underscoring every sentence with a line on the schoolmaster's sleeve. The emphasis was helped by the speaker's square wall of a forehead, which had his eyebrows for its base, while his eyes found commodious cellarage in two dark caves, overshadowed by the wall. The emphasis was helped by the speaker's mouth, which was wide, thin, and hard set. The emphasis was helped by the speaker's voice, which was inflexible, dry, and dictatorial. The emphasis was helped by the speaker's hair, which bristled on the skirts of his bald head, a plantation of firs to keep the wind from its shining surface, all covered with knobs, like the crust of a plum pie, as if the head had scarcely warehouse-room for the hard facts stored inside. The speaker's obstinate carriage, square coat, square legs, square shoulders – nay, his very neckcloth, trained to take him by the throat with an unaccommodating grasp, like a stubborn fact, as it was – all helped the emphasis.

'In this life, we want nothing but Facts, sir; nothing but Facts!'

> From *Hard Times – Gradgrind and Bounderby* by Charles Dickens

TIMED WRITING *(15 minutes)*

1 Write your own short description of a place or a person using some of the techniques for exaggeration you have studied. You could include:

- strong dramatic language
- repetition of language and/or structures
- lots of detail.

2 Then annotate your work to show which techniques you have used and why.

Now work with a partner. Share the description you have just written and discuss the choices you have made.

↘ Action stations

Another useful technique that writers use to entertain is to create action. Action scenes can help to change the pace, build up a sense of excitement and lead up to a climax.

ACTIVITY 5

1 Quickly read the extracts from *Across the Atlantic*, below, and *Silent Hunters of the Deep*, on page 34. Decide which parts:

  a speed up the action   c create suspense

  b slow down the action   d lead up to a climax.

You could record your findings in a chart like this:

Effect	Example	Reason for choice
Speeds up the action.	Pace quickens – turf becomes a blur –	Because of the short sentences and dashes.

In this extract a pilot describes trying to take off carrying more fuel than his plane is used to carrying.

Across the Atlantic

I keep my eyes fixed on the runway's edge. I *must* hold the plane straight. One wheel off and the *Spirit of St Louis* would ground-loop and splinter in the mud. Controls begin to tighten against the pressure of my hand and feet. There's a living quiver in the stick. I have to push hard to hold it forward. Slight movement of the rudder keeps the nose on course. Good signs, but

more than a thousand feet have passed. Is there still time, still space?

Pace quickens – turf becomes a blur – the tail skid lifts off ground. I feel the load shifting from wheels to wings. But the runway's slipping by quickly. The halfway mark is just ahead, and I have nothing like flying speed – the engine's turning faster – smoothing out – the propeller's taking better hold – I can tell by the sound. What r.p.m? But I can't look at the instruments – I must hold the runway, not take my eyes from its edge for an instant. An inch off on stick or rudder, and my flight will end.

The halfway mark streaks past – seconds now to decide – close the throttle, or will I get off? The wrong decision means a crash – probably in flames – I pull the stick back firmly and – *the wheels leave the ground*.

> From *Across the Atlantic* by Charles Lindbergh

This extract describes a shark attack.

Silent Hunters of the Deep

On 8 December 1963, Rodney Fox was competing in the South Australian Spearfishing Championships, having won the title the previous year.

Fox was in superb form, drifting, gliding, spearing his quick **elusive** targets with the practised ease of a born competitor. With an hour left, he looked likely to win the title again. He was one kilometre (1100 yards) offshore, drifting in for a shot at a **dusky morwong**, sure of the kill, his finger tensing on the trigger, when something huge hit his left side – 'it was like being hit by a train' – knocking the gun from his hand and tearing the mask from his face. His next impression was of speed, surging through the water faster than he had ever done, a gurgling roar in his ears, and of the easy, rhythmical power of the shark, holding him as a dog does a bone.

With his right arm he clawed for the shark's eyes; it released its grip and Fox instinctively thrust out his right arm to ward it off. The arm disappeared into the shark's mouth, **lacerating** the underside on the bottom row of teeth. As the horrified Fox jerked it out, the arm caught the upper jaw. **In extremity** men do amazing things: Fox, terrified of the open **maw**, tried to bear-hug the shark, to wrap his arms and legs around the **abrasive** skin, to **get a purchase** away from the teeth. It did not work – the shark was too big for him to hug.

He suddenly realised another need even more urgent than fending off the shark – air. He pushed away, kicked for the surface, gulped one breath and looked down on a scene that burnt itself into his memory. His mask gone, his vision blurred, he floated in a pink sea, and a few metres away was a pointed nose, and a mouth lined with razor sharp teeth, coming at him.

In desperation, Fox kicked with all his force at the shark. It was a **terminal gesture**, pointless, useless – but it worked: the shark turned from Fox, lunged for the buoy tied to his belt, swallowed it whole, then plunged for the deep.

> From *Reader's Digest*

Word bank

elusive: good at getting away
dusky morwong: type of fish
lacerating: tearing
in extremity: in extreme circumstances
abrasive: rough and scratching
get a purchase: get a hold
terminal gesture: final act

2 Now read the extracts again, but more closely, and identify how the writers create the sense of action. Look for examples of the following:

- long sentences with lots of clauses
- short sentences with simple clauses
- short clauses that appear on their own as if they are sentences
- paragraphs made up of single sentences
- use of action verbs
- use of dialogue
- delaying the climax to build up suspense.

Creating action in your own writing

Below are the first and second drafts of an action scene from a story about a girl called Carla. She has lost something she had borrowed without permission.

How has the writer improved the second draft so that the action scene is more effective and interesting? Look at the bullet list in Question 2 above to help you.

First draft

Carla ran home from school to search the house before her mother got home. She turned the living room upside down looking for the medal. She would be in real trouble if it wasn't back in the drawer when her mother came to look. She still hadn't found it when she heard her mother come in.

Second draft

Carla flew in the door, hot and panting from her desperate sprint home. Scarcely pausing for breath, she dumped her bag and ran into the living room, where she began her frantic search. She pulled the sofa out, throwing off the cushions and hunting down the sides, before whirling round to the sideboard and yanking open every drawer and door, creating havoc as she burrowed through the clutter. Where could she have put it? Could it have fallen on the floor? She was on her knees, lifting up rugs and peering under furniture when she heard the sound.

Footsteps.

A key in the latch.

Carla froze. Now she was in for it.

TIMED WRITING   *(15 minutes)*

Now try some of the same techniques yourself to create an action scene for one of the situations below.

- A flock of birds flies into the school dining hall during the busiest part of lunchtime. Things get chaotic.

- A character is running a race and is in the lead. In the last stretch, a competitor begins to catch up from behind.
- You are on your bicycle and the brakes fail as you are wheeling down a very steep hill. There is a river at the bottom of the hill.

Working with a partner, read each other's pieces of writing.

a Explain to your partner how you tried to build up a sense of excitement and suspense.
b Discuss suggestions about how you could improve your own writing.
c Work with your partner in the same way on their piece of writing.

TIMED WRITING *(30 minutes)*

Copy and complete the planning grid below to help you write about one of the following subjects.

a Describe a real or imagined occasion when you were caught doing something you should not have been doing. Use a range of techniques to build up suspense for your readers. Make sure you:

- choose and build up detail carefully
- vary the length of sentences
- describe your response or feelings
- build up to a climax.

b Imagine you are taking part in the national finals of your favourite sport. Describe the last minutes of the game, concentrating on writing effective action scenes. Make sure you:

- vary the length of sentences and clauses to slow down or speed up the action
- use paragraphs of single sentences for dramatic effect
- use action verbs
- delay the climax to create suspense.

Ideas for the opening sentence(s):

Ideas for the ending:

Setting:

Characters:

Descriptive words and phrases:

B Writing to inform, explain, describe

Writers may inform someone of the ingredients in packaged food; they could explain how a boat sank in a newspaper report; they might describe a house in an estate agent's report. In this section, you will explore a range of non-fiction texts and use the skills that you learn to create your own pieces of writing.

Unit B1 will help you pull together information for particular audiences. You will learn how to organise your writing so that it is presented clearly and is easy to scan.

Unit B2 will help you explain something effectively so that your readers know exactly what and how they should be doing something, and why. You will also learn to order an explanation so that it is easy to follow and how to use the passive.

Unit B3 will help you create vivid pieces of descriptive writing. You will learn how to develop your key idea, create variety with synonyms and explore subjective and objective points of view.

Copy and complete the chart below. Decide under which heading in the chart each of the following examples should go. You may feel that some belong in more than one category. For example, a travel brochure informs people about holiday destinations and prices; it may also describe resorts and hotels. Then add some more examples of your own.

- Ingredients listed on a tin of baked beans.
- Guide book for visitors to your area, town or city.
- Railway timetable.
- Travel brochure.
- Letter to parents about a school trip.
- Review of a new CD.
- Account of a visit to the Taj Mahal.
- Make-up tips.
- Missing-person poster.
- Newspaper report of a football match.
- Recipe for pancakes.

Inform	Explain	Describe
Ingredients listed on a tin of baked beans		

B1 Inform

When you inform people about something, you pull together relevant information, present it clearly to get their attention and make it easy to scan. In this unit, you will look at different examples of writing to inform, such as a survey and an advertisement, and you will write pieces of your own.

You will focus on:

● planning and including subheadings and topic sentences

● organising your paragraphs

● using language targeted for a specific purpose and audience.

Look at the examples you included under the heading 'inform' in the activity on page 38. You probably had all or some of the following:

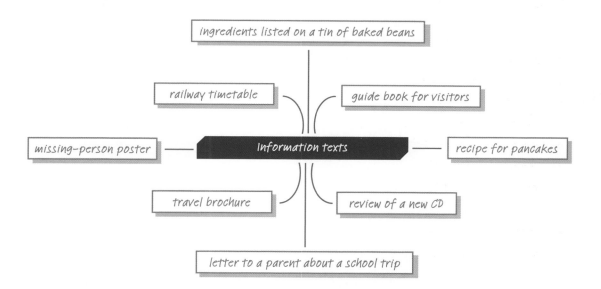

ACTIVITY 1

1 Thinking about the examples you thought of for the activity on page 38, code the statements below to show whether they are:

- true for all the examples (TA)

- true for some of the examples (TS)

- false for all the examples (FA)

- false for some of the examples (FS).

a Information is set out in tables, graphs and/or diagrams.
b The text entertains the reader.
c Subheadings and different fonts are used to set information out clearly.
d The text is not written in full sentences.
e The text is written in full sentences.
f Instructions/commands are given.
g The passive voice is used.

2 Work with a partner. Create a set of guidelines for recognising writing that informs. The guidelines should tell readers the features to look for. You could use the headings below to help:

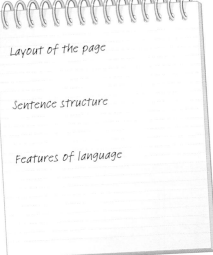

Layout of the page

Sentence structure

Features of language

↘ Getting it sorted!

When your main purpose is to inform, you need to make sure your writing is organised so that the reader can find the information easily. Ways in which writers do this include:

- use of headings and subheadings

- organisation of paragraphs

- use of topic sentences to introduce a paragraph

- use of cohesive words, which link sentences and ideas

- layout of the text.

↳ Paragraphs

Now you are going to look at some guidelines for organising informative writing into helpful paragraphs. Read the annotations which point out the features in the paragraph below.

Subheading says what the paragraph is about and helps the reader locate information.

This topic sentence introduces the main gist of the paragraph.

All the information is on a similar theme – handling – and relates to the topic sentence.

Handling your iguana

Young iguanas should be handled only for a few minutes daily, as anything more than this is stressful. Being out of the cage for any length of time will result in the body temperature dropping and a cool iguana will not thrive. When alarmed or threatened, iguanas, particularly young iguanas, will jump erratically. In the wild, they leap from branch to branch and away from danger. In captivity, the result may be an unpredictable leap from a shoulder. Be prepared for these sudden leaps and handle the animal securely and close to the ground, as serious injuries can occur.

Use of similar structures starting with 'In ...' and contrasting ideas like 'wild' and 'captivity' helps to link ideas.

Use of the pronoun 'they' referring back to 'young iguanas' links the sentences.

> From the petcare.com website

ACTIVITY 2

1 Copy the chart below. Read the sentences below, which are taken from a text about tarantulas that was originally in two paragraphs. Using the chart, decide how you would organise the sentences back into two paragraphs. Each paragraph should deal with a different aspect of looking after tarantulas.

TRP
p17

Paragraph 1	Paragraph 2

Tarantulas

a   Tarantulas are excellent climbers and, no matter what kind of cage you use, a secure top is a must.

b   Tarantulas are predators and will eat just about any living animal they can capture and kill.

c   If you cover the air holes with a screen, be sure to use a metal screen that the spider cannot chew through easily.

d   Feeding once a week is enough and larger spiders can be fed every other week.

e   Larger tarantulas sometimes eat small snakes, lizards and mice.

f   This will both keep the spider in and help keep poking fingers and other potentially harmful harassment out.

g   Crickets, most beetles, grasshoppers, earthworms, moths and other animals are acceptable.

h   Several small air holes in the top and/or sides will provide enough oxygen for the spider and at the same time help maintain air circulation and humidity.

i   Removing uneaten food after a day or so will help keep the cage clean.

j   Spiders will not overeat.

k   Avoid wasps and bees, since they could harm the spider, and do not use insects from areas that might have been sprayed to get rid of pests.

l   Almost any kind of container can be used to house your tarantula – an aquarium, plastic shoe box, even a gallon glass jar will provide a home for a young tarantula.

m   You should not offer food every day.

> Adapted from the concentric.net website

2 Decide which sentence you would choose to be the topic sentence for each paragraph. Ask yourself these questions:
   a   Does a clear topic sentence emerge for each paragraph?
   b   Are there any sentences which only make sense when paired with another sentence?
3 Now give each paragraph a subheading.
4 Compare your decisions with a partner's work. Did you make the same decisions?
5 Compare your decisions with the original text from your teacher. Does your structure reflect the original? If it differs, explain how.

↘ Planning your own writing

Below is a brainstorm diagram created by a pupil who was asked to write an informative text about her home town.

a   Give your recommendations for organising the ideas into paragraphs.

b   Suggest subheadings and topic sentences for the piece of writing.

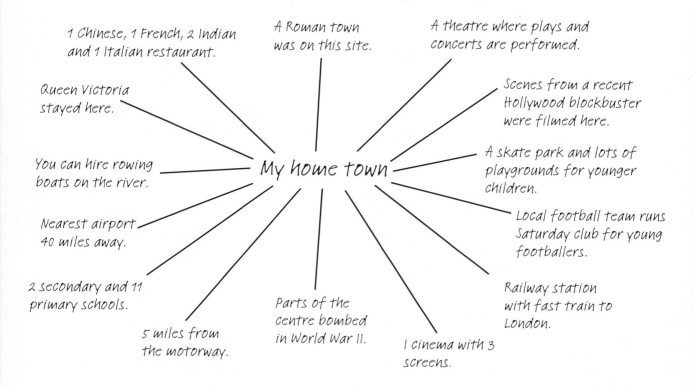

Organise your ideas in a planning grid like the one below, which has been started to help you.

My home town	
Subheading 1	The history of my town.
Paragraph 1	All the details of what has happened in the town in the past.
Topic sentence 1	My home town has a very long history.
Subheading 2	Transport connections.
Paragraph 2	
Topic sentence 2	
Subheading 3	Lots of entertainment.
Paragraph 3	
Topic sentence 3	
Conclusion	

TIMED WRITING *(20 minutes)*

1 You are going to write a short guide for visitors to your school. First, make a list or create a brainstorm diagram of all the information you might want to include. Try to include at least twelve things.

2 Look carefully at your list or diagram and decide on:
  a how you will organise the information into paragraphs
  b helpful sub-headings
  c possible topic sentences.
  Organise your ideas in a planning grid like the one you used on page 43.

3 Then write up your notes into three well-organised paragraphs. Make sure that:
  ● similar information is grouped together
  ● you have a clear topic sentence to introduce each paragraph
  ● you use subheadings to help your readers find what they want to know quickly.

↘ Purpose and audience

As with other kinds of writing, you will have to think carefully about the **purpose** (what the writing is trying to do) and the **audience** (who it is aimed at) when writing to inform. Considering different purposes and audiences will involve thinking about the content, layout and language of your writing. For example:

Style and tone: Is the writing informal or formal? Does it use slang? Does it use specialist terms only a certain group of people might understand? Is it complex or easy to follow?

Content: What sorts of detail are included? How might these be of interest to a particular audience?

Layout: Does the layout make it easy to follow? Does it try to appeal to a particular type of reader and/or create a particular impression through use of colour, fonts and pictures?

ACTIVITY 3

TRP
p17

1 Read the four web texts on the next few pages. All of them inform the reader, but they have different purposes and audiences.

2 Copy the chart below into your books. For each piece of writing, decide on the purpose and the audience, and make a note of them in your chart.

3 Discuss your decisions with a partner.

4 Then complete the 'Reasons' column with the things that helped you decide. Give as many reasons as you can.

Text	Purpose	Audience	Reasons
The Feathers Hotel			
Skateboard review			
Veterinary nurse			
Television survey			

Welcome to the Feathers Hotel

Market Street . Woodstock . Oxfordshire . OX20 1SX

The Feathers Hotel, situated in the centre of historic Woodstock just a few miles from the University city of Oxford, is a privately owned 17th-century country town hotel. Originally five separate houses, the hotel boasts character and charm with antiques, log fires and traditional English furnishings.

Woodstock

... an ancient Royal Borough in England's historic heartland

Woodstock is one of England's most beautiful and famous country towns. Constructed largely from Cotswold stone, its buildings date from the 12th century. It is host to a wealth of interesting shops, restaurants and historical buildings – including the Oxfordshire County Museum.

Situated only eight miles from 'The Dreaming Spires' of the historic University of Oxford, on the edge of the spectacular Cotswolds and huddling next to the gates of Blenheim Palace – home of the 11th Duke of Marlborough and the birthplace of Sir Winston Churchill, Woodstock has much to offer its visitors.

Woodstock is just one hour's drive from London Heathrow, Birmingham and Cheltenham – Shakespeare's Stratford is a mere 45 minutes away.

'A wonderful 17th century inn ... the restaurant fare is out of this world'
Traditional Homes

> From the feathers.co.uk website

Ballistic Skateboards

Looking for something new? Try Ballistic Skateboards. We got a few boards from them and passed them out to a few of our best taste testers, this is the feedback we got.

If you're looking for pop this is a deck for you (and check this, it seems to keep its pop for a long time). The boards tend to sport a big nose and tail and a super slick, high-gloss bottom. Graphics run dark and gloomy and the 7-ply maple decks come in $7\frac{1}{2}$, $7\frac{3}{4}$ and 8 inch. By all reports they are worth checking out.

Liar Skateboards

In a blind skate test, it's hard to distinguish one deck from the other. Am I lying? I don't think many people would disagree with me.

Given this little titbit, then, it would be important for a company to either establish a vastly popular and market-able image or a reputation for quality. Despite a self-proclaimed predilection for the opposite, the small, South Carolina based Liar Skateboards seems to be making an honest effort at attaining both these lofty goals.

The Liar board I skated measured approximately 32 x $7\frac{3}{4}$ inch with a 7 inch nose and a $6\frac{3}{4}$ inch tail. Despite the fact that it was not sanded pomade slick and compressed to streamlined perfection, the deck didn't feel clunky and awkward. This board had substance, giving some flex without feeling like a joggling board. Each pop felt solid, but after some wear there seemed to be the potential for future sluggishness.

If you are the type of person that prefers aesthetics to art, Liar graphics may appeal to you. This deck featured simple and clean style. Emblazoned on the all-white deck was a bold green 'Liar' logo that resembled a graffiti artist's interpretation of a digital display. The paint job wore away to the wood after one long slide, however.

Truth be told, the Liar deck can take the Pepsi challenge with about any deck. So, if you're looking for a small company that can provide quality, it's out there.

What does it take to be a veterinary nurse?

Veterinary nurses work alongside vets, dealing with the day-to-day care of hospitalised animals and helping with operations, cleaning teeth and taking samples. Veterinary nurses' work includes:

- getting patients ready for operations
- monitoring a patient's breathing, heart rate and body temperature during operations
- claw clipping, wound checks and suture removal
- scaling and polishing teeth under general anaesthetic
- making sure that hospitalised animals have food and water
- monitoring anaesthetics (under a vet's instruction)
- taking samples of blood, skin and urine
- running clinics like puppy socialisation and weight clinics
- triage (assessing patients before a vet sees them)
- stock taking and ordering drugs
- positioning animals to be x-rayed, then developing the films for the vet to look at.

It's a good idea to work part time or as a volunteer at a vet's surgery so that you have relevant experience before starting veterinary nurse studies. You could get experience at:
- a veterinary clinic • a kennels or cattery • an animal welfare centre • a riding stables.

To become a veterinary nurse you usually need to have 5 GCSEs or Standard Grades (C or above, or grades 1–3). These should normally include English and physics, chemistry or biology. You can also do specialised courses such as a BTEC National Diploma, Certificate in Animal Care or BVNA pre-veterinary nursing course. To be a fully trained nurse you need to take one of the following courses:
- NVQ level 2/3 in veterinary nursing (2 years)
- BSc in veterinary nursing (4-year degree course).

Veterinary nursing is an interesting job with varied work but it can be poorly paid with long hours or shift work, so you need to be dedicated. As well as caring for animal patients, the job involves helping with operations and clinics so you need to keep up to date with current practices. It's a good idea to get as much practical experience as possible before applying for a veterinary nurse course.

> From the bbc.co.uk website

Children / parents: television in the home – a national survey

The typical household surveyed has two working television sets in the home. The survey found that while most parents report that on a typical day their child watches two or more hours of television, more than three-quarters do not believe that the child is spending too much time watching TV, and a majority think that television has done their child more good than harm.

Parents provide consistent evidence that their concern is not how much their children watch but what sorts of programming they are watching. Sixty-six per cent of the parents report rules about watching television. Of those, 40% don't want their children to watch certain programmes, 36% permit viewing only after completion of homework or chores, 20% only permit watching at certain times of the day, and 17% limit the number of hours.

Of the possible influences on children, 61% of the parents surveyed said they were most concerned about what their children are exposed to on television.

Most parents (82%) believe that it is somewhat or a lot harder to raise children these days compared to when they were growing up. A substantial majority (79%) provides quite a bit or a great deal of supervision over their children's activities. More than half report providing a great deal or quite a bit of supervision over the television programmes their child watches (66%), their child's school work (62%), the clothes their child wears (58%), their child's choice of friends (53%), and the music their child listens to (50%). School work is most often cited as the thing that needs the most supervision, followed by television and choice of friends. Parental involvement in children's television viewing is reflected in the parents' report of the frequency with which they watch television with one of their children.

Conducted for the Annenberg Public Policy Center of the University of Pennsylvania under the Direction of Kathleen Hall Jamieson

> From *Children/parents: television in the home – a national survey* by Peter D. Hart Research Associates.

TIMED WRITING *(30 minutes)*

1 Re-read the piece of writing you created about your school for the activity on page 44.
2 Re-write the paragraphs for a completely different audience, such as:

- a new pupil
- a new head teacher
- a cat burglar
- an estate agent who might sell the buildings.

Before you write, decide on the changes you will make to the style and tone, the content, and the appearance and layout.

When you have written your paragraphs, annotate them to show the changes you have made to suit your new purpose and audience, and discuss your changes with a partner.

B2 Explain

Writing to explain shares many of the features of writing to inform. In a nutshell, writing to inform gives readers the 'what' – important facts and things they might need or want to know – whereas writing to explain goes beyond the 'what' and may tell readers: **how** to do something, **how** something works or **why** something happened.

However, some texts can do both. For example, a newspaper story about a football match will **inform** readers about who won and who scored, and may possibly **explain** such things as why the match was important and how key decisions about players were made.

In this unit, you will create your own piece of explanatory writing.
You will focus on:

- recognising the features of explanation
- organising your ideas well
- using the passive.

 ## Features of writing to explain

ACTIVITY 1

1 Read the extracts on page 50 and, using the list below, identify some of the features of explanatory writing.

 FEATURES OF EXPLANATORY WRITING

- Clearly organised into paragraphs.
- Complex as well as simple sentences are used.
- Connectives such as 'before', 'next' and 'once' show the chronological order in which things happen.
- Connectives such as 'because', 'since', 'owing to' and 'as a result of' show cause and effect.
- The passive emphasises things and actions rather than people.
- Words such as 'may', 'seem to' and 'apparently' show when something is not proven.
- Explanatory writing can be in:
    - the first person, (I), if you are explaining something you did or experienced
    - the second person, (you), if you are explaining how to do something
    - the third person, (he, she, it), when you are explaining something outside your own experience.

Plummeting cows

A Japanese fishing boat had been sunk by a falling cow in the Sea of Okhotsk off the eastern coast of Siberia. The shipwrecked crew were plucked from the sea, claiming that cows had fallen from the sky and one of them had gone straight through the deck and hull, capsizing the vessel.

The fishermen were arrested for suspected **marine insurance fraud**, but freed after Russian and Japanese investigators found out that the story was true. Russian soldiers based on the island of Sakhalin had used an army transport plane to rustle a herd of cattle. Once airborne, the cattle moved about the aircraft, throwing it off balance. To avoid crashing, the crew drove them out of the large loading bay at the tail of the aircraft at 20 000 ft (6000 m).

> From *The Daily Mirror*

Word bank

marine insurance fraud false claim of accident at sea to get insurance money
sonar system of detecting shapes under water based on sound pulses
telepathic able to read people's minds

Dolphin doctors

It has been known for many years that dogs, cats and other animals can play a vital role in maintaining a healthy mind, and healthy body by association. They help anxious people to relax, at least partly because their affection is unconditional – it bears no relation to sex, age, size, colour, shape or appearance. Whether dolphin therapy works on exactly the same basis, or whether dolphins have an extra-special quality that we have yet to identify, no one really knows.

Intriguingly, dolphins seem to be able to recognise depression or illness in people. Researchers have found, time and again, that dolphins have an uncanny ability to home in on the people who most need help, even when there are other people in the water. Again, no one can explain how they are able to do this. One possibility is that, if they are highly sensitive to energy fields, they may be able to pick up subtle abnormalities in the fields of people with health problems. Another is that they can pick up problems with their sophisticated **sonar**, which may enable them to 'see' inside the human body. It may even be psychological: it is often suggested that dolphins are **telepathic** (they certainly seem to be more intuitive than most people), and so they may be able to read minds and emotions.

> From *Book of Dolphins* by Mark Carwardine

TIMED WRITING *(20 minutes)*

Write two or three paragraphs to explain one of the following:

● how to survive lunch time in your school

● how to play your favourite sport or game well

● how you got into trouble about something.

To help you, look back at the list of explanatory writing features on page 49.

Putting your ideas in order

You will have noticed in the list of explanatory writing features on page 49 that two of the ways of ordering ideas mentioned were chronological ordering and by showing cause and effect. In this section, you will look at some ways of structuring your sentences and achieving order in your writing so that readers can easily follow and understand what you are saying.

Chronological connectives

When you are writing an explanation that depends on chronological order, it seems unnecessary to say that you need to take care to organise your ideas in the right order. However, there are different ways of doing this to make your writing interesting and your meaning clear to your readers – using chronological connectives is one of them.

ACTIVITY 2

1 Read the following sentences and identify the words that make the order clear.
  a Before opening the door, he stopped to listen.
  b I packed my books into my bag and then set off for school.
  c As the volcano erupted, people were fleeing the city.
  d Once I was sure it was cold enough, I carefully removed the car's radiator cap.
Notice how the words that tell you the order of events are used to make the sentences more interesting.
2 Compare the original sentences with the following versions.
  a He stopped to listen. He opened the door.
  b I packed my books. I set off for school.
  c The volcano was erupting. People were fleeing the city.
  d I checked the radiator was cold enough and next I took the cap off.
Which versions are more interesting to read?

 REMEMBER

Chronological connectives can help to make your writing:
→ clearer by showing when things happen
→ more interesting because they encourage you to create complex sentences with a variety of beginnings and clauses.

ACTIVITY 3

Read the extract below, which explains the history of St Petersburg, a city in Russia. The words that help establish the chronological order have been removed and put in a box. Put the words back into the text in a way that makes sense.

TRP
p19

- following
- after
- since
- during
- during
- today
- after
- following

St Petersburg

St Petersburg, Russia's second city with a population of five million, was renamed Leningrad and even Petrograd _____ its Communist rule, which spanned the greater part of the twentieth century. Situated in the country's European north-west, the city is young by Russian standards; founded in 1703, St Petersburg celebrated its 300th anniversary in 2003. In 1703, Peter I captured the area of present-day St Petersburg (originally a Swedish fortress) and ordered the construction of a new city and fortress on the site, named after his patron saint. His aspiration was for

St Petersburg to become westernised, considering it 'a window into Europe'.

Emperor Nicholas II decided to change the Germanic name St Petersburg to the Russian name of Petrograd in 1914, following Russia's declaration of war on Germany. In 1918, Moscow replaced Petrograd as the new capital of Russia. _____ Lenin's death in 1924, the city was given the name of Leningrad in honour of the great leader.

_____ World War I when the Russian Baltic provinces were lost, Leningrad grew in importance because of its position as the Soviet seaport nearest to Western Europe.

_____ World War II, Leningrad was the site of heavy fighting during a siege by German forces from 1941– 4. Over one million residents died from this military action or from the proceeding onset of disease and starvation, and over 10 000 buildings were ravaged.

Rebuilt _____ World War II, Leningrad resumed its original name St Petersburg _____ the collapse of Communism in 1991. _____ its early years, this was a legendary city, rich in mythical stories and legends told in a St Petersburg style. _____, St Petersburg houses over 1700 public libraries.   The largest, M.E. Saltykov-Shchedrin Library, was founded in 1795 and now houses almost thirty million volumes. St Petersburg is now a centre for manufacturing and shipbuilding for Russia.

> From the www.pilotguides.com website

Cause and effect

Showing cause and effect is an important part of explaining how or why something happens. For example:

- a naturalist explaining why birds migrate for the winter
- an environmentalist showing the effect of greenhouse gases
- a teacher explaining why a pupil is in detention
- a builder explaining why new drains are needed
- a scientist writing up a lab report
- a police officer explaining why someone was arrested.

ACTIVITY 4

1 Think of all the examples that you can where writers might need to show cause and effect, for example in Geography or Science books.
2 Compare your examples with a partner. See who can build up the longest list.

TRP
p19

ACTIVITY 5

Connectives showing cause and effect

As with chronological ordering, there are connectives that will help you to show cause and effect in a more interesting and effective way.

1 Look at the words and phrases below, which help to establish cause and effect in your writing.
2 Write some sentences to use each one effectively. If you get stuck, use a dictionary or thesaurus. Here is one example to help you.

> *In the light of recent concerns about mobile phones and radiation, it seems logical to ban them in school.*

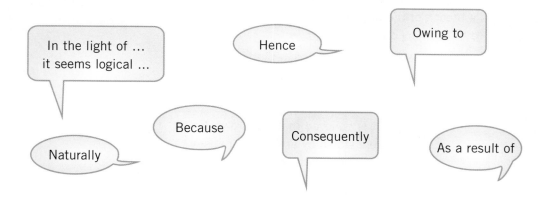

↘ Using the passive

When writing to explain, writers often use the passive. They do this because it's a way of:

- leaving out things they **don't** want to tell
- emphasising what they **do** want to tell
- making writing sound impersonal and formal.

ACTIVITY 6

1 Read the following sentences.
    a The stolen Crown Jewels were found under a bush in the park.
    b The stolen Crown Jewels were found by retired postman Mr Pat under a bush in the park.
    c A man found the stolen Crown Jewels under a bush in the park.

2 Decide which one:
    a emphasises the Jewels
    b emphasises the man who found them
    c appears to give equal emphasis to both.

When should I use the passive?

The passive can be used in formal explanations

The passive is often used in fairly formal texts, such as when writing up a science experiment or describing a procedure. This is because it stops unimportant detail, such as who did what, getting in the way of the more important explanation and helps to make the text absolutely clear.

The passive is sometimes used to give authority or make something sound official.

Phrases such as 'It is believed that ...', 'It is commonly felt that ...' and 'It has long been known that ...' are often used to add authority to a statement and give the impression that something is true.

Read the statements in the speech bubbles. Why do you think they are in the passive?

> It is felt that school uniform is a breach of the human right to be an individual.

> It has long been known that smoking is dangerous.

> It is believed that the Crown Jewels were stolen by anti-hunt protestors to draw attention to their cause.

ACTIVITY 7

1   Write one or two paragraphs explaining why schools set homework. Try to use examples of the passive where you feel it would be effective. Here are some examples to get you started:

> Homework has been set at this school since ...

> It has long been known that ...

2   Explain your choices to a partner or your teacher.

The passive can be used when the writer is unwilling to say, or is unsure about, who is responsible for something

For example, you will often see newspaper reports on tricky situations written in the passive. This is because the reporters may not have all the information or may need to avoid seeming to blame someone.

The passive can also be used with 'by' if the writer wants to mention the person who did something

For example:

> *The play **was written by** Shakespeare.*

> *A drowning man **was rescued by** a local teenager.*

ACTIVITY 8

1   Read the following extract from a news report about the twin towers disaster in New York. Examples of the passive have been highlighted and annotated.

Fatal delays that trapped crowds

Failure to warn may have cost hundreds of lives

By Ed Vulliamy and Jane Martinson in New York

Although the twin towers had been targeted by terrorists as recently as 1993, there seemed to be no clear evacuation plans. Marvin Jackson, a survivor of the first tower to be hit, said he did not think there were any evacuation plans in place. 'I don't think anyone anticipated that this would ever happen again', he said.

The passive here creates a formal tone.

K.D. Srinivasan, a technician at Deutsche Bank asset management, had been allowed to enter his office in Canal Street at 9am on Tuesday, almost 15 minutes after the first explosion. Soon after taking his coat off, colleagues started talking about seeing bodies. 'Then we heard the explosion and the building started to shake. I just didn't want to stay there. Nobody told us to leave.'

The mayor, Rudolph Giuliani, admitted that, while the second building to be hit had had 'a chance to clear out', the first had not.

Brookfield Properties, the Canadian company that manages the World Financial Centre, denied that its handling of the disaster had been flawed. It said that all emergency plans had been implemented, including the evacuation of tenants and employees.

In these examples the passive allows the writer to avoid saying who was responsible or laying blame.

> From *The Guardian*

2   Now read these extracts from the texts you read on page 50. Examples of the passive have been underlined. In each case, decide why the writer has chosen to use the passive and what effect has been achieved.

Plummeting cows

A Japanese fishing boat had been sunk by a falling cow in the Sea of Okhotsk off the eastern coast of Siberia. The shipwrecked crew were plucked from the sea, claiming that cows had fallen from the sky and one of them had gone straight through the deck and hull, capsizing the vessel.

The fishermen were arrested for suspected marine insurance fraud, but freed after Russian and Japanese investigators found out that the story was true.

> From *The Daily Mirror*

Dolphin doctors

Another is that they can pick up problems with their sophisticated sonar, which may enable them to 'see' inside the human body. It may even be psychological: it is often suggested that dolphins are telepathic (they certainly seem to be more intuitive than most people), and so they may be able to read minds and emotions.

! REMEMBER

→ Look at the list of explanatory writing features on page 49 to help you plan your piece of writing.

→ Think about how you might use the passive.

→ Put your ideas in a clear, logical order.

→ Show cause and effect, if possible.

→ Use a planning grid to organise your ideas before you start writing.

> From *Book of Dolphins* by Mark Carwardine

 TIMED WRITING   *(45 minutes)*

Choose from one of the following topics.

a   Write an article for a magazine aimed at teenagers explaining how to cope with exam stress.

b   Imagine you have flooded your house. Write a letter explaining the incident to the insurance company, being careful to go into detail but not to admit blame if you can help it!

B3 Describe

Descriptive writing can include a whole range of purposes and audiences and you will find it in both fiction and non-fiction texts. The main purpose of any descriptive writing is to give readers a mental picture of what they are reading about. In this unit, you will write your own descriptive account.

You will focus on:

- writing from different points of view
- creating a vivid mental picture
- adding variety by using synonyms.

ACTIVITY 1

Below are three pieces of text that all describe the same house. Read them and match each text to one of the following purposes:

a   a surveyor's report for prospective buyers

b   an estate agent's advertisement

c   a description from the autobiography of a former resident.

A period semi-detached house on a lively street. Many original features remain, including sash windows and fireplaces. Ground floor comprises entrance hallway, a large living room, dining room, kitchen and utility room. First floor accommodation includes three spacious bedrooms plus boxroom/bedroom four and family bathroom. There is stairway access to a large attic. At the rear of the house is an 80 foot garden with mature trees and a pond. Price: £162,000.

The house I grew up in seemed huge to me. There were dark corners to hide in – under the stairs, in the vast kitchen cupboards or behind all the years of junk piled up in the boxroom. Once my brother and I daringly climbed the forbidden stairs to the attic to explore. It was an enchanted – and scary – cave to us, with cobwebs draped in every corner and creaking floorboards. Another time I remember well was when he persuaded me to climb one of the garden trees with him – it was a twisty old willow and not that hard to climb, but I slipped on the slimy moss covering the old branches, and fell in the pond.

The house is in need of some renovation. The original window frames are rotten on the ground floor and will need replacing. There is damp in the rear ground floor walls that will need specialist treatment. We recommend that the wiring is given a safety inspection by an electrician, as it appears to have been installed some time ago. The attic flooring is weak and should not be walked on without extra boards being laid down. The roof is slate and appears to be sound and free from leaks.

⭷ Purposes and points of view

As you can see from Activity 1 on page 57, the way something is described can create very different impressions. These impressions will depend on the intended purpose and audience of a text and on the writer's point of view.

When writing a description, you may wish to be either subjective or objective in your point of view.

REMEMBER

→ **Subjective** means giving a personal point of view, in which the feelings and reactions of the writer are an important part of the impression being created.

A subjective description of your cat might include how sweet she was when she was a kitten, how you like her to sleep on the end of your bed and tricks she has got up to. It would emphasise your feelings about your pet, as well as the animal's characteristics.

→ **Objective** means standing back and trying to give a factual, unbiased account.

An objective description of your pet cat might give her colour, age and weight. It might also describe her eating habits, where she likes to sleep and whether she gets along with other animals. These are all facts that anyone could observe.

ACTIVITY 2

Decide whether the examples below would be more likely to use subjective or objective description.

a a description of a flowering bush from a gardening handbook
b a description on a missing-person poster
c a description of a celebrity's outfit from a fan magazine
d a description of a holiday in a letter to a friend
e a description of a car's condition by a mechanic
f a description of a pudding on a restaurant menu
g a description of a character in a novel.

Using subjective and objective details

A good way to get started with descriptive writing is to think about the subjective and objective details you might wish to use. You could use a chart like the one below. The example here uses the idea of the house from Activity 1 on page 57.

Subjective	Objective
● house seemed huge to me as a child	● 3 bedrooms
● lots of good places to hide	● old
● attic was frightening like a cave – the floorboards sounded spooky	● attic floors creak
● memories of climbing the willow tree – the slimy green texture – falling off	● big rooms
	● big cupboards in the kitchen
	● trees
	● pond

TIMED WRITING *(15 minutes)*

1 Choose one of the following topics and create your own chart of subjective and objective descriptive details:
   ● your best friend
   ● your primary school
   ● your least favourite lesson
   ● your favourite meal
   ● a storm.

2 Write a short objective description and a longer subjective one using the ideas from your chart.

Share your work with a partner. Discuss the choice of detail in your work. Decide on other details you could have included.

REMEMBER

→ You can make your writing more vivid by including details which refer to all five senses and by using metaphors and similes.

→ You can use objective ideas in subjective description, but you can't use subjective ideas in objective description!

↘ What's the big idea?

Successful descriptive writing is built around a key idea or impression, which will be the most important picture or feeling you want to create in your readers' minds. For example, if you are describing a person, do you want readers to get the impression that the person is scary, loyal, scruffy, kind or selfish? You could, of course, combine the ideas – someone could be both scruffy and kind.

TRP
p20

ACTIVITY 3

1 Read the three following extracts. For each one, decide what key idea or impression the writer is trying to convey.

2 Identify three or four details that help create the key idea. The first one has been done for you.

TRP
p21

Key idea: power and determination of the giant squid

This suggests that the squid is an horrific and frightening creature and shows its strength and determination.

This adverb makes the description dramatic and shows the powerlessness of the mother to help.

This detail emphasises the power of the prey, showing that squids will tackle even a large whale.

This detail adds to the idea of determination – the squid hung on until death. It also creates an impression of horror.

'Ten Arms and a Giant's Eye'

We know from eye-witness accounts that the giant squid feeds on whales. In October 1966, two lighthouse keepers at Danger Point, South Africa, observed a baby southern right whale under attack from a giant squid. For an hour and a half the monster clung to the whale trying to drown it as the whale's mother watched helplessly. 'The little whale could stay down for 10 to 12 minutes, then come up. It would just have enough time to spout – only two or three seconds – and then down again.' The squid finally won and the baby whale was never seen again.

Giant squid have been seen in battle with adult whales too. In 1965, a Soviet whaler watched a battle between a squid and a 40-ton sperm whale. In this case neither was victorious. The strangled whale was found floating in the sea with the squid's tentacles wrapped around the whale's throat. The squid's severed head was found in the whale's stomach.

> From 'Ten Arms and a Giant's Eye' by Lee Krystek

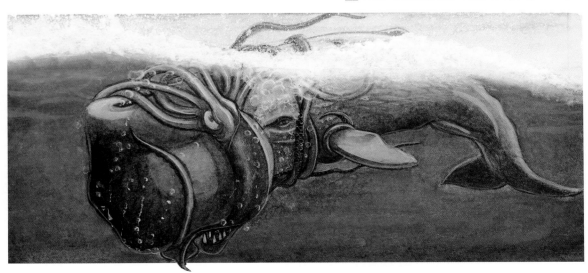

Key idea: This writer grew up during the Second World War. In this text, he describes his reactions to the idea of having a baby in the family.

Alarms

I was fifteen and babies horrified me. The smell of talcum powder or of washing drying indoors had always plunged me into misery – another new baby to turn the house upside down and punish me for the sin of just being there. But there hadn't been a baby for years and I thought all that was finished with ... and then, one day, I saw a carton of food for 'expectant mothers' half hidden on the larder shelf and I realised that my mother was pregnant.

Nobody had mentioned it and I had managed not to see her increasing size, but now the bulge in her pinafore, which I had tried to ignore, was just what I had feared. I kept the guilty knowledge to myself.

This was no way to welcome a brother. I woke up one morning and was told that my mother, taken to a nursing home in the night, had given birth to a baby boy. I pretended it was news but I could not pretend to be happy – unlike another morning soon afterwards when I shouted downstairs to ask what the score was. My father called up, 'A hundred and eighty-five for the loss of three of ours.' The Battle of Britain and my brother Frank came almost together.

> From 'Alarms' by John Gordon

Key idea: This text describes a man's experience of being followed by, he believes, the secret police in Soviet Russia.

Kiev and the KGB

I took a mental note of the car number-plates behind the hotel, and that evening it was one of these which framed itself in my mirror as I drove south into the suburbs: Kiev 75–86. Once it had gauged my speed, the white Volga saloon lingered back in a way which I was soon to recognise, tucked behind a lorry four cars behind. I might have shaken it off – it assumed I was unaware of it. But by now I was worried. I had no idea why I was wanted. Had they traced me back to meetings with dissidents in Moscow or Leningrad? I didn't know. Every minute or two the white shadow in my mirror would ease out as if to pass its covering lorry, then slide back. Once, in distraction, I overshot some red traffic-lights, and the Volga accelerated and did the same. A policeman tried to flag it down. It took no notice and swerved in close behind me. I saw a short, dark man seated in front, and a thin, fair driver. They fell back again instantly, concealed behind a truck.

> From 'Kiev and the KGB' by Colin Thubron

TIMED WRITING   *(15 minutes)*

To practise developing key ideas, you are going to create contrasting descriptions of the same thing using a planning grid to help you. A grid will help you to brainstorm details that build up different impressions about your subject. As an example, the planning grid below has been created to plan for writing two different impressions of the same teacher.

Choose one of the following topics to write about:

- a party as a fun experience and as a boring evening
- your bedroom as a haven of peace and privacy, and as a claustrophobic prison
- a dog as a perfect pet and as a scary predator
- rain as a good thing and as a bad thing
- a practical joke as good fun and as something you are ashamed of.

Use a planning grid like the one above to brainstorm the details you would include under each key idea.

Share your work with a partner. Discuss the choice of detail in both your pieces of work. Decide on other details you or your partner could have included.

Subject: teacher Key idea 1: teacher is threatening	Key idea 2: teacher is interesting and clever
• very tall – seems to tower over you	• a real presence – you sit up and take notice when he walks in
• loud voice – makes the windows rattle like thunder	• controls the class so everyone behaves and learns
• boring – he rambles on and on	• he loves his subject – you can tell by the way his eyes light up and he can always give you extra information if you ask
• sarcastic remarks – everyone's nervous he might pick on them	• very sharp sense of humour even if it sometimes turns on the pupils
• harsh marker – hard to get good grades; dread getting work back	• a good grade from him is really worth something
• old – can't relate to pupils.	• he taught some of our parents too – it feels like he belongs in our community and it makes parents' evenings a laugh!

↘ Using synonyms

When you are writing a description, your choice of words can make the difference between a dull, repetitive piece and a lively, interesting read. To help you create writing that is varied and vivid, even though you are describing only one thing, you need to make the words work hard and will probably need to use synonyms.

❗ REMEMBER

→ Synonyms are words with similar meanings, for example, shut/close.

→ Antonyms are words with opposite or contrasting meanings, for example, love/hate.

ACTIVITY 4

1   Complete a chart like the one below with synonyms for each word.

Word	Synonyms	
bright	shining glowing sparkling	
soft	comfortable springy fluffy	
quiet		
happy		
hot		
loud		

2   Share your chart with a partner. Did you find different words?
3   Get together with another pair. Create a group chart of all the synonyms you have thought of.
4   Work in groups. Use a thesaurus to add more synonyms to your chart.
5   Now try to find antonyms for the same words.

TRP
p21

63

ACTIVITY 5

The writer of the text below has had some trouble finding synonyms to express the key idea of darkness.

1 Re-write the text to make the description more interesting and varied, using some synonyms for darkness. Some synonyms to help you get started are given in the box below, but you can also use your own ideas. Remember that you can use words in their different forms, for example 'gloom' (noun) or 'gloomy' (adjective).

- gloomy
- black
- sombre
- dreary
- miserable
- grey
- shadowed
- depressing
- dusky

> The thing I remember most about my grandparents' house is the darkness. You walked into a dark hallway with old, darkened wallpaper. The furniture was all heavy and dark. It cast dark shadows in the corners. The windows were small and the net curtains added to the darkness. My grandfather himself dressed in dark colours – he always looked to me as if he were on his way to a funeral. He never said much and his expression suggested that his thoughts were dark, too. My grandmother would, I think, have liked more light and colour around to relieve the darkness that sat upon the house like a wet, heavy dark blanket.

TRP
p21

2 Compare your text with the original and annotate the reasons for your changes. Share your ideas with a partner.

TIMED WRITING *(15 minutes)*

Using the chart you compiled for Activity 4 on page 63, write a short descriptive paragraph on one of the topics below. Use as many synonyms as you can to convey your key idea.

- A hot summer's day on the beach.
- A quiet corner of a garden.
- A happy moment when you got something you had wanted for a long time.
- A noisy dinner hall at school.
- A soft sofa you are relaxing on.

↘ Getting it organised

Organising descriptive writing can be done in a range of ways. For example:

- chronologically if, for example, you are describing an event
- spatially to show where things are or what they look like from your point of view if, for example, you are describing a place or an object
- as a journey to take readers through events or places as, for example, a walk through a house from front door to garden.

ACTIVITY 6

1   Read the three extracts below and on p65 and decide how they have been organised. The first one has been done for you.

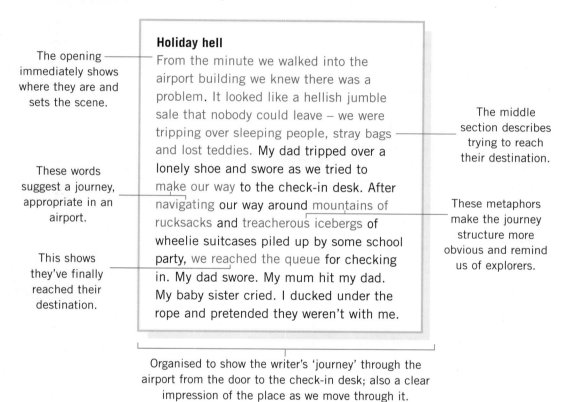

The opening immediately shows where they are and sets the scene.

These words suggest a journey, appropriate in an airport.

This shows they've finally reached their destination.

Holiday hell

From the minute we walked into the airport building we knew there was a problem. It looked like a hellish jumble sale that nobody could leave – we were tripping over sleeping people, stray bags and lost teddies. My dad tripped over a lonely shoe and swore as we tried to make our way to the check-in desk. After navigating our way around mountains of rucksacks and treacherous icebergs of wheelie suitcases piled up by some school party, we reached the queue for checking in. My dad swore. My mum hit my dad. My baby sister cried. I ducked under the rope and pretended they weren't with me.

The middle section describes trying to reach their destination.

These metaphors make the journey structure more obvious and remind us of explorers.

Organised to show the writer's 'journey' through the airport from the door to the check-in desk; also a clear impression of the place as we move through it.

The problem with exams

At one o'clock exactly we were told to open our test papers. My hand shaking, I turned the page. Just as we had been told, I began by reading the question and paused to reflect before reading the question again. The only problem was, I didn't get it. Around me, people had already begun to write. What was wrong with me? Why couldn't I think? I looked at the clock, back at the question and finally at the floor in despair. I couldn't do it. Finally, I began to write, hoping that it would all make sense in the end.

It was worth it!

From the back of the stadium, the band are no bigger than ants, but it doesn't matter. There are huge screens towering over us that show us every tiny detail. Anyway, there is a wall of a man in front of me – I couldn't see over or round him even if the stage were only five feet in front of me. I notice that his jeans are slipping down and I hope they last the evening. If they don't, I might see more than I paid for. Even if I can't see the band, the sound system shakes the whole county, which means we can all hear just as well as the lucky ones at the front.

2 Decide why each writer has organised their description in the ways that they have.

3 Discuss what might be the best way to organise a piece of descriptive writing about:
   ● a haunted house
   ● building a snowman
   ● waking up in the morning
   ● someone you know well.

 TIMED WRITING   *(45 minutes)*

Write a description of one of the subjects below:
   ● your first friend
   ● your hero
   ● a real or imagined time when you were in danger.
   ● an animal you fear
   ● a typical teenager's bedroom

Copy and complete the planning grid below to help you plan your writing.

Title:

Purpose / your point of view:

Key idea:

Organisation of other ideas:

Subjective details:

Objective details:

Appropriate synonyms / antonyms:

Writing to persuade, argue, advise

Writers use many forms of writing to persuade, argue or advise. For example, they might create a letter to persuade people to donate money to a good cause; or they might write a speech to argue for something; or they might produce a leaflet to advise teenagers on how to deal with bullying. In this section, you will explore a range of non-fiction texts and use the skills that you learn to create your own pieces of writing.

Unit C1 will help you to think about the audience in writing to persuade. You will learn how to anticipate their reactions so that your persuasion is more effective. You will also practise how to use precise words to influence your readers' feelings and how to use particular writing techniques to grab their attention.

Unit C2 will help you to think about the language you use in writing to argue. You will also practise how to build up an argument and how to balance fact and opinion.

Unit C3 will help you to understand your readers' concerns – an important starting point in writing to advise. You will also practise using presentation devices and how to choose words and phrases which will give your advice a stronger impact.

It's a good idea to collect examples of texts that persuade, argue and advise on topics that interest you. Look at the post that comes through your door and at posters, magazines, newspapers, and look on the Internet to get a feel for the different audiences being addressed and the purposes and approaches used.

The chart below shows examples of texts that persuade, argue or advise. Copy the chart and complete it with the details of the texts you have collected. This will help you think about how the texts are put together.

Text	Audience	Purpose	Type of language	Source
Leaflet persuading people to donate money to beat child poverty.	Adults	● To increase donations. ● To create feelings of compassion.	● Informal language creates empathy. ● Sympathetic tone appeals to the heart.	Save the Children leaflet
Letter to local newspaper about plans for a skateboard park.	Local community	● To present the proposal. ● To win support for the proposal. ● To reduce support for competing proposals.	● Formal language gives a certain tone of authority.	Letters page of local newspaper
Guidance booklet for new Year 7 pupils.	Pupils	● To advise on life in their new school.	● Formal language inspires confidence. ● Friendly tone wins support.	School

C1 Persuade

When you persuade someone, you present them with a convincing case to make them do or believe something. In this unit, you will look at a speech, a brochure and leaflets that persuade and you will create a piece of persuasive writing.

You will focus on:

- anticipating your readers' reactions
- choosing language to influence feelings
- choosing an appropriate tone
- using writing features that are particularly effective in writing to persuade.

↘ Anticipating your readers' reactions

When you want to persuade someone to believe or to do something, it is very important that you anticipate their reaction before you start. Take the following situation: You want to go to town on Friday night. Thundering Megadeath is appearing at the local football ground. However, on your last visit to a concert you were late home and your mother had to pay for an expensive taxi. She also discovered that you were with a school friend she doesn't like. How would you go about persuading your mother in these circumstances? First, it is important to think of all the possible objections she might have and what you can say to counter them or even reassure her. You could plan your persuasion in a spider diagram.

Concert ends at 10; will come straight home			Friend's father driving

Home late   Expensive taxi

Went with friend mother did not like — **Concert – want to go!!!**

Going with girl Mum likes

Written out, it might look like this:

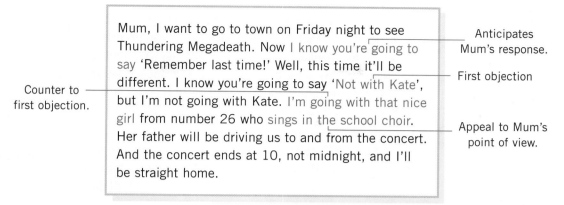

Anticipates Mum's response.

First objection

Counter to first objection.

Appeal to Mum's point of view.

Mum, I want to go to town on Friday night to see Thundering Megadeath. Now I know you're going to say 'Remember last time!' Well, this time it'll be different. I know you're going to say 'Not with Kate', but I'm not going with Kate. I'm going with that nice girl from number 26 who sings in the school choir. Her father will be driving us to and from the concert. And the concert ends at 10, not midnight, and I'll be straight home.

TRP p33

ACTIVITY 1

1 Think of another similar situation and the audience you would want to persuade.
   a Make a spider diagram mapping out all the possible objections to what you want.
   b Then add a persuasive reply to each objection.
2 Using your diagram, write a paragraph to persuade your chosen audience to agree to what you want.

 REMEMBER

Remember to choose an appropriate style and tone. The style and tone for the concert example is conversational and informal because it is a conversation between close family members. In other situations, for example a letter to the local newspaper, you would need to be more formal.

Think carefully about the audience you are writing for. You need to consider:
→ how formal you need to be
→ whether the use of humour is appropriate
→ how much factual information you should include.

Getting the right tone and structure

To get the tone right, you need a clear understanding of who your audience are and what their views are. Then you can concentrate on the most appropriate way to address them. Consider this example. Rajni is a Year 9 pupil. Some of her class would like to go to a theme park for their end-of-year treat. However, Rajni and her friends think that a local hands-on museum is a more appropriate choice for a school-based treat. She has been chosen to make a presentation to try to persuade the class to accept her ideas. Read her speech and the annotations on page 70 to see how she sets the tone and structures her speech to win over her audience.

Starts by recognising the role of the teachers – this will get them on her side.

This phrase shows sympathy for the other proposal and tries not to upset its supporters.

One of the first hints of a better proposal, which is followed up later.

Direct, punchy appeal to audience to introduce Rajni's proposal.

Tries to persuade her audience with the promise of exciting things to do.

Presents the other proposal first.

Shows understanding of the other proposal.

Anticipates negative reaction to her proposal.

We are lucky in our class to have this chance of an end-of-year trip. If our teachers were not willing to give up their own time to organise the trip and go with us, we wouldn't be able to go. Because they have been so co-operative, we need to think carefully about our destination – we don't have to go to a place that is just superficially attractive.

Darren and Wesley have suggested Waterside Adventure Park. It's an attractive choice. The rides are thrilling and the food's great. But I don't need to tell you that! I think everyone in the class has been at least once for a birthday or other treat. We have all screamed on the Lightning Waterfall and enjoyed the Superburgers. Even with £14.99 entrance fee and the cost of food and transport, it's a great day out.

So why go again? Why not try something new, something we wouldn't ask for as a birthday treat?

Fellside Discovery Museum will give us the chance to see things we have learned about in Science in action. It's not a stuffy museum with strict rules. It has a hands-on approach where we can do experiments and feel sensations we've only read about before. You don't just read about the functions of the liver – you get one out and have a look! You don't just draw pictures of the stars – you pilot your own spacecraft through them! And all for £6.99 each, including a healthy lunch – it's excellent value for money.

We've all seen plenty of theme parks. Let's make this year something special and challenging!

The tone is slightly formal with some informal parts to appeal to an audience of teachers and pupils.

ACTIVITY 2

Re-read Rajni's speech and consider how she has tried to persuade her audience. Then copy and complete the chart below.

a   In the first column, write out all the objections Rajni anticipated to her proposed activity.

b   In the second column, write down Rajni's response to each objection.

c   In the third column, write down some of the words and phrases she used to persuade her audience.

TRP
p34

Objection	Response	Persuasive words and phrases

You might not have voted for Rajni's plan, but you can see how she set about her persuasion. She did not start with her own ideas, but with the other proposal. She admitted how attractive it was and then looked at its advantages and disadvantages. Then she used those points to build her own case.

REMEMBER

→   When you want to communicate your ideas effectively, show that you understand the opposing ideas before you express your own. The objections you will have to overcome will vary, depending on your audience.

→   Remember to choose the right tone for the situation – formal or informal – to win your audience over to your way of thinking.

ACTIVITY 3

Your local council is proposing to develop an area of natural woodland into an adventure playground for teenagers.

1   Copy the chart on page 72. Complete the chart by writing your ideas on what the reactions of each group might be and the likely reasons for their reactions.

Group	Reaction	Likely reasons for
Members of a local woodland preservation group	We strongly oppose this proposal.	The playground will destroy the woods and wildlife.
Local home owners		
Local shopkeepers		
Residents of a local old people's home		
Local young people		

2 Now write the first paragraph of an article for a local newspaper in which you try to persuade one of the local groups of the benefits of the scheme.

 TIMED WRITING *(20 minutes)*

Imagine the following situation. Your school has been left £10 000 in the will of a local businessman who was an ex-pupil. The money can be spent on any aspect of school life. You have been asked to submit your ideas on how to spend this windfall to the head teacher and school governors.

1 Plan how you will present your proposal. You may find a planning chart like the one for Activity 3 is helpful. Remember to consider your audience, their likely objections and an appropriate tone to address them. Plan your responses to the objections.

2 Now write your proposal to persuade your audience to choose your ideas, building in all the features that you have planned.

↘ Choosing words to influence feelings

The particular words you choose for your writing are vitally important. Choosing the right words will help to persuade your readers to see your point of view or get them on your side. To do this, you will need to consider your audience carefully because you have to appeal to their feelings and stir up their emotions.

Read the following example. It is a sentence from a leaflet campaigning against blood sports. Notice the choice of words.

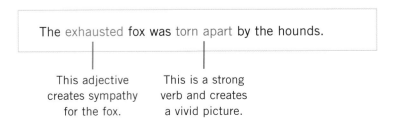

The exhausted fox was torn apart by the hounds.

This adjective creates sympathy for the fox.

This is a strong verb and creates a vivid picture.

ACTIVITY 4

a   Read the sentences in the following chart and note the highlighted words.

b   Work out the type of persuasive text in which you might find the highlighted words.

c   Copy and complete the chart by choosing a more precise word than the original one. The first one has been done for you.

Original text	Type of text	More precise word
The oil escaped from the tanker.	environmental report	oozed
I am asking you to improve your behaviour.		
The animals have drops placed in their eyes.		
Some pupils are dropping litter in the corridors.		

Emotive language

Emotions are similar to feelings. So when you choose words to influence people's feelings, you are using emotive language.

REMEMBER

A careful and precise choice of words can influence how people feel and persuade them to accept your point of view.

ACTIVITY 5

Read the following passage and think about the highlighted words. The writer is putting forward a clear point of view, but the choice of words could be better.

The amount of dog's droppings is causing a mess on the pavements of our area. What should be a pleasant walk down an attractive avenue has become a game of missing piles of dirt, which sticks itself and its smell to your shoes. — *lottery*

However, I don't blame the dogs; it is their owners who must be blamed. They need to remember their responsibilities. Why can't they carry a scooper to clear up their dog's mess? Why should we have to often clean the paths outside our houses? It's time we residents fought back and asked these people to accept their responsibilities as well as their rights to own a pet. — *homes*

1   Replace the highlighted words with more emotive words. Choose words that will give readers strong feelings about the subject and persuade them to accept the writer's point of view. Two suggestions have been made for you.

2   Share your ideas with a partner. Discuss in detail how their changes make you feel.

↘ Choosing words to show feelings

Your choice of words can also give away your own feelings on the issue you are writing about. For example, you may be angry, disappointed or worried. The words you choose will also affect the tone of your writing, so again you need to think carefully about what is appropriate for your particular audience. The right tone is vital for effective persuasion. You want your ideas to be read, not thrown away in anger or disgust!

ACTIVITY 6

Copy the chart below, which lists some words for common emotions. Each of the words also conveys a particular tone that you might want to use in some pieces of writing.

Emotive word	Verb	Noun
hate	abhor	abhorrence
envy		
fear		
worry		
regret		

Think of as many similar meanings (synonyms) as you can for each word in the chart. Notice that all of these words can be used as verbs or nouns. For each word you have thought of, make sure you list it as a verb and as a noun. You could use a dictionary or thesaurus to help you.

TIMED WRITING *(35 minutes)*

Your local council has given permission for a town park to be sold off for office buildings. The park is a little run-down, but it is the only park in the town centre. Write to persuade your local council to invest in improving the park rather than going ahead with the building scheme. Copy and complete the planning grid below to help you plan your writing.

1 Make sure that you identify your own point of view precisely. This will help you to maintain a consistent viewpoint, choose the best words for the appropriate style and tone, and therefore produce a more effective piece of persuasive writing.
2 Remember to list all the factors that might affect the council's decision, such as the reactions of local residents and businesses. This will give you a better idea of their problems, points of view and the objections they might raise.
3 Decide on the form of writing that would be most appropriate. You might consider:
   ● an open letter to the councillors
   ● an illustrated fact sheet on advantages and disadvantages
   ● an article in the local newspaper addressed to the council.
4 You may find it easier to fill in the title after you have made the rest of your decisions.
5 When you start to write, try to establish the style and tone you want straightaway. You don't want to upset the councillors!

Title:

Your own viewpoint:

The reasons for your viewpoint:

Factors affecting council's point of view:

Objections the council might raise:

The form of writing:

Formal or informal tone:

Words to create the appropriate tone:

Words to influence feelings and opinions:

↘ Features of persuasive writing

You are already familiar with some of the features that writers use to make their writing more persuasive. The following features are effective even in just one or two sentences.

FEATURES OF PERSUASIVE WRITING

- **Deliberate exaggeration to influence feelings**

  > The quantity of food in school dinners must increase. Pupils are <u>starving</u> in afternoon lessons.

  The pupils might be hungry, but the word 'starving' implies they might die through lack of food, which is clearly an exaggeration.

- **Adjectives giving a strong positive or negative impression**

  > It is a <u>bustling</u> resort with a <u>lively</u> night life.

  > The resort has <u>dangerous</u> roads and <u>hazardous</u> beaches.

  These two sentences could be about the same resort. All the underlined words create strong impressions, but they are positive in the first sentence and negative in the second.

- **Alliteration for effect**

  > The <u>s</u>nake <u>s</u>lithered <u>sm</u>oothly thr<u>ough</u> the <u>s</u>ilent n<u>ig</u>ht.

  Alliteration is often achieved by repeating consonants to create an effect. The repetition of the 's' in this sentence makes the sound often associated with snakes and the movements they make. Alliteration can also be achieved by repeating vowels – here the long 'oo' and 'i' sounds add to the impression of a long, slithering shape and the slightly spooky nature of the whole scene.

- **Exclamation marks to draw attention**

  > What a colourful beach there is opposite this hotel!

  This sentence, and the scene it describes, would seem much less colourful without the exclamation mark.

- **Rhetorical questions to involve readers**

  > Can you wait to take a break at the Hotel La Bamba?

  Rhetorical questions, like this one, do not require an answer, but they still stimulate a silent response from readers.

REMEMBER

Using adjectives is not only a good idea for descriptive writing, but can also help you to be more persuasive.

ACTIVITY 7

1 Write a sentence of your own to illustrate each of the five features on page 76.
2 Share your sentences with a partner and discuss the persuasive effects of each feature.

Combining features for persuasive writing

The features you studied on page 76 can be combined even in a relatively short text to give the appropriate tone for a very effective piece of persuasive writing.

ACTIVITY 8

a Read the text below. It is a piece of writing aimed at persuading people to take their holidays on the North-East coast, rather than in some of the better known English resorts.

Alliteration creates a happy feeling.

Exclamation mark emphasises the point.

Positive adjectives create an appealing atmosphere.

It may not be as bubbly or breezy as Blackpool. It may not have the genteel charms of Torquay. Nor the international surfing reputation of Newquay. Nor the singing shingle beaches of Brighton. But it does have all of these somewhere: breezy at Alnmouth, charming at Seahouses, surfing at Tynemouth and the odd spot of shingle among the soft and golden sands.

But there is so much else too! The castle and beach at Bamburgh, which must be as dramatic and powerful as any in Europe. Seaside golf courses as challenging as any in Scotland. Hidden coastal hamlets that offer the visitor cosy and inviting inns serving fresh and appetising local food. The birdwatchers' paradises at Buddle Bay and Druridge Bay. The jewel of Lindisfarne, which is the most celebrated religious site in England.

Can these attractions be beaten anywhere in England? Surely it is only a matter of time before you book up!

- Informal style with incomplete sentences and missing verbs is appropriate to the holiday mood.
- Upbeat tone gives positive impression and more credibility for the claims about the North-East coast.

b Re-read the text with a partner. Find examples of the following features. A few examples have been annotated for you.

- Positive adjectives.
- Exclamation.
- Rhetorical questions.
- Alliteration.
- Exaggeration for effect.

ACTIVITY 9

1 Write out four examples for different features of persuasive writing that you picked out in Activity 8. Consider why they are so effective and persuasive.

2 Now think of a visitor attraction in your area. For example, it might be a museum, theme park or national heritage site.

3 Write an advertising leaflet of no more than 100 words to persuade people to visit your chosen attraction. Use the four features you have picked out, but use them wisely. They are more effective if you don't overdo them.

 TIMED WRITING *(35 minutes)*

A new housing development is being built in your area. Your head teacher is keen that the children of the families who move in choose to attend your school.

Write the text for a leaflet to be given to all the house buyers to persuade them that your school is the best possible choice for their children. Remember it is the parents who will make the decision.

Copy and complete the planning grid below to help you plan your writing.

a Decide whether the style should be formal or more relaxed and conversational. Your decision will affect the style of your sentences.

b Choose the appropriate tone – it will need to be positive, but not desperately pleading. This will affect the language you choose to use.

c Plan the layout of the leaflet and think about how this will affect the length and organisation of the paragraphs.

Title:

The positive reasons for choosing your school:

Factors affecting the parents' points of view:

Concerns about the school the parents might raise:

Formal or informal tone:

Words to create the appropriate tone:

Words to influence feelings and opinions:

Introduction:

Message in each paragraph:

Message in the conclusion:

C2 Argue

When you write to argue a particular case, you present your readers with a convincing case to try to win them over, just as you do with writing to persuade. However, in writing to argue it is particularly important that you present a balanced case, considering the arguments on both sides before coming to your conclusion.

You will focus on:

- using connectives to link your ideas
- balancing fact and opinion
- structuring your argument.
- building up an argument
- considering cause and effect

↘ Structuring your ideas

A good argument consists of a point of view that is clearly set out, supported by evidence and reached after considering all the information and other viewpoints. So it is important to use words and phrases that will help you structure what you want to say.

Using connectives

Connectives are words and phrases which help you to link your ideas and compare one point of view with another. Below are some examples of connectives:

- but
- however
- alternatively
- on the other hand
- on the contrary
- consequently
- as a result
- despite this
- whereas
- nevertheless
- in spite of
- equally
- because
- this leads to
- the opposite

ACTIVITY 1

TRP
p36

Read the notes below. In each case, turn them into one or more sentences using one of the connectives above. There may be more than one possible answer.

a we could spend the money on new disco equipment – we could give it to charity

b the skate park may have to be closed – vandals are causing a lot of damage

c cycling keeps you fit – it's dangerous to cycle on busy roads

d foxhunting should be banned – that would cause unemployment in rural areas

e chat rooms can be a fun way to communicate with people – they can be dangerous for children

TRP
p36

f young people spend a lot of time watching television – they can become overweight and unable to make friends

Building up an argument

ACTIVITY 2

The speech below was given by a Year 9 pupil to the School Council. The Council was making a decision on what to do with the money raised on the next non-uniform day. This pupil argues that the money should go to famine relief in Africa.

This speech is an example of how to build up an argument clearly and concisely. Read the speech and answer the questions in the annotations.

How many of you walked a round trip of eight miles carrying a heavy load of water before you came to school this morning? How many of you have serious doubts about getting a reasonably sized meal sometime today? Does your father or mother have to walk twenty miles to a feeding station to carry home a heavy bag of rice to make sure your family will eat tonight?

> In the first paragraph the writer uses rhetorical questions. What effect do you think these questions have on the audience?

These are the basic facts of life for many children in Africa as we sit here today. Without money and support to help improve their land and farms, children of our age will go to bed hungry. They may even die from lack of food!

> In the second paragraph the writer suggests what might happen if these people don't get money. What effect do you think this has on the audience?

We could forget about them. We could vote for Dean's suggestion and spend the money we raise on new school disco equipment so that some of the older boys can learn how to be DJs.

> In the third paragraph, why do you think the writer refers to this idea for using the money? How might the audience react to this, in contrast with the idea of sending the money to Africa?

On the other hand, we could donate the money we raise on the next non-uniform day to famine relief in Africa. You might think it wouldn't make any difference to people's lives. However, we know that it would. According to the charity's annual report, 75p in every pound goes direct to people in Africa. It is used to help rural communities get clean water, grow food and set up small workshops to enable them to earn some money. Here is the report – you can read it for yourself!

> Find two connectives in the fourth paragraph. Notice how they mark clear stages in the argument and link them together.
> What factual information does the writer refer to in paragraph 4?

We can make a real difference by sending this money to famine relief. We have so much and these people have so little.

> The conclusion is short and punchy and reveals the writer's own feelings. Can you describe these feelings in two or three words?

↘ Balancing fact and opinion

Successful writing to argue will show a balance between the use of facts and the writer's opinion, both of which must be relevant to the argument. For example, the sentence

> Mount Everest is the highest mountain in the world.

is a fact, but the following sentence is an opinion:

> To climb Mount Everest must be the most challenging task in mountaineering.

Here the writer's opinion is based on the fact, but it is nevertheless an opinion. Other mountains may not be as high as Everest, but they may be more difficult to climb.

An argument can be centred on personal opinions, but these should be based on facts that can be proved. If you don't check out the facts and your audience can prove that the supposed facts you have used are wrong, your argument will be badly damaged.

You can decide whether an opinion is valid or not by looking at whether it is backed up by

> So many people climb Mount Everest these days that it is becoming a rubbish dump. This week a team of environmentalists reported collecting more than 1.2 tonnes of waste, including empty tins, batteries, ropes, used oxygen cylinders and broken ladders.

ACTIVITY 3

evidence or reasons, for example:

1 Read this newspaper article about the problems at a skate park.
   a Make a list of any facts in the article.
   b Make a list of any opinions in the article.
2 Which words in the text helped you to decide what was fact and what was opinion.

Vandalism threatens future of skate park

Didcot's skate park may be permanently closed down only 15 months following its opening after vandals sliced through a metal safety barrier with a disc grinder.

Police investigating a catalogue of damage believe the grinder was also used to cut up a skateboarder's £200 mountain bike.

So far this year, vandalism and other problems occurring in parks and recreation grounds in Didcot have cost the town council £80 000.

Councillors warned that the matter will be discussed at a council meeting next week and a decision to close and fence off the skate park might only be weeks away.

Despite appeals for help to prosecute offenders – which have not resulted in any names or information to help police – PC Roger Foster said he believed the vandals were not necessarily skateboarders. 'Local residents have heard noises in the skate park late at night, after the skateboarders have left so we know that some damage has been caused by other people.'

Skateboarders accused BMX riders of cutting down safety posts and damaging concrete ramps and safety rails to adapt the skate park for their two-wheeled sport.

> From *The Oxford Times*

↘ Cause and effect

As we have seen, you can build an argument by using evidence to present your point of view. The evidence is the facts that have **caused**, or led to, the particular issue about which you wish to argue. You can then use these facts as a basis for your opinions, developing them to show the **effects** of the issue in question.

Look at the following three points, which could be related to the problem of violence at football matches.

- There is less violence at football matches now.
- Sales of alcohol are limited.
- There is more control over ticket sales.

These simple statements of fact in short sentences don't really show the writer's argument clearly. However, exactly the same ideas could be presented in a complex sentence, like this:

> Since the sale of alcohol was limited and there has been more control over ticket sales, there has been less violence at football matches.

Notice that the facts about alcohol and ticket sales are now presented as the causes of violence, and are quite clearly linked to the opinion that they have the effect of stirring up violence.

↘ Presenting an argument

Look at the way the following argument on compulsory PE at school has been presented and developed.

Why should we all be forced to change into shorts and take part in games and exercises?

- We have Human Rights laws. Is compulsory PE not against these laws?

- We have choices in many other areas of the school curriculum – why not this one?

- The idea that you should 'Do what you're told – it's good for you' is not good enough for today's pupils.

Notice the use of rhetorical questions and the use of an appropriate tone, emotive words and expressive adjectives. The writer has also linked ideas well to make the argument more effective.

ACTIVITY 4

Re-arrange each set of three simple sentences below to link the causes and effects into one complex sentence. The first one has been started for you.

a
- Some young children are seen as a threat by older people in our area.
- They meet together in large groups in the town centre.
- There is a lack of out-of-school activities for young people in our town.

> *Older people in our area .... because they meet together .... and because of the lack of ....*

b
- Cycling to work or school is the best way of travelling short distances.
- More cycling means less traffic pollution in our town.
- Cycling is a good way to maintain fitness.

TIMED WRITING *(20 minutes)*

Write similar short arguments on the following topics. You should decide whether you will argue *for* or *against*.

- No school on Fridays.

- No chips in the school canteen.

When you have finished, share your work with a partner. Tell your partner two positive aspects about their writing and make two suggestions for how they might improve it.

Structuring your argument

When you are writing your own argument text, you will need to think carefully about how to organise the points you want to make. Below are two ways in which you could do this and examples of each. (Note that these are only first drafts and the writers will need to do more work on them.)

Introduction	
Paragraph 1:	point in favour
Paragraph 2:	point in favour
Paragraph 3:	point against
Paragraph 4:	point against
Conclusion	

Introduction	
Paragraph 1:	point in favour
Paragraph 2:	point against
Paragraph 3:	point in favour
Paragraph 4:	point against
Conclusion	

People get very passionate about fox hunting. It is a very controversial issue and there have been many marches and demonstrations both for and against it. Some people believe it is cruel, while others believe it is a part of country life and should continue.

Some people believe that foxes are pests. Farmers in particular often support fox hunting because they say it helps them keep the fox population under control. They believe that foxes are a threat to lambs and chickens.

Another argument is that fox hunting brings employment to rural areas and that if it is banned a lot of people will lose their jobs.

However, people who are against fox hunting feel that it is cruel and unnecessary because fox hunters kill foxes only for 'sport'.

In addition, anti-hunt supporters argue that foxes are not pests at all. They claim that foxes eat mainly small wild animals, rather than farm animals.

On balance, I am in favour of fox hunting because I think there are strong arguments for it.

People get very passionate about fox hunting. It is a very controversial issue and there have been many marches and demonstrations both for and against it. Some people believe it is cruel, while others believe it is a part of country life and should continue.

Some people believe that foxes are pests. Farmers in particular often support fox hunting because they say it helps them keep the fox population under control. They believe that foxes are a threat to lambs and chickens.

However, anti-hunt supporters argue that foxes are not pests at all. They claim that foxes eat mainly small wild animals, rather than farm animals.

Another argument is that fox hunting brings employment to rural areas and that if it is banned a lot of people will lose their jobs.

In contrast, anti-hunt supporters say this is an exaggeration and very few jobs would actually be lost. Even if a lot of jobs were lost, I think this would not justify allowing such cruelty to continue.

On balance, I am against fox hunting. If we claim to live in a civilised society, we should ban it immediately.

ACTIVITY 5

Now it's your turn to write an argument text. When you do this, you might find it helpful to follow the steps below:

1 Decide on a topic

For this activity, choose a topic from the speech bubbles to write about, or think of your own. Note that each topic is in the form of a question – so you know at once that there will be more than one point of view about the answer. If you choose to write about your own topic, put it into a question so that your readers know that they will be hearing arguments about a particular point of view.

Is gambling harmless fun or a destructive menace?

Does vegetarianism offer a healthier lifestyle?

Is it safe for children to use chat rooms?

Does television help to educate us or merely waste our time?

Are celebrities paid too much money?

2 Think about what you want to say and/or gather information

You can use your own ideas, but also think about how you might find out more about the topic you are going to write about. For example, you might find information by:

- talking to people
- reading newspapers and magazines
- visiting the library
- searching the Internet.

3 Organise your ideas/information

As you have seen, grids, charts and spider diagrams are a useful way of organising information. Choose a method that suits you. For example:

Is gambling harmless fun or a destructive menace?	
Fun	A menace
Lottery – doesn't cost much; a lot of money goes to charity	People get addicted to scratch cards – winning a lot of money can ruin people's lives

4 Decide on your point of view

Having thought about the topic, talked to people, searched the Internet, etc., what do you feel about the topic? Make up your mind about your point of view before you start writing.

5 Structure and write your argument

Now use the material from your grid, chart or spider diagram to write out a first draft of your argument. When you have completed the first draft, read it through and see if you can make any improvements or changes, and check that everything is clear.

You could also ask a partner to read it and offer you feedback on what you have written and suggestions for improvements.

ACTIVITY 6

The article below was written by an educational journalist. It is aimed at parents thinking about the choice of secondary schools for their children. Although the writer gives some general information, he also presents his views on how parents should choose schools for their children and the issues that can arise. He has chosen to structure his argument by first presenting all the points in favour of choice and then all the points against.

If your child is in a state junior school then he or she will be in a feeder school for a particular comprehensive school. However, parents do not have to take this choice of comprehensive school even if they intend to keep their children in the state system. The law in this country allows parents to opt to send their children to schools other than their local comprehensive.

Many parents consider that choice is a sensible idea because they think that they should have the right to choose their children's school. They may not just be influenced by a school's exam results. They may prefer, for example, to send their children to a school with inspiring music or language departments or with excellent sports facilities.

A further argument put by parents is that this essential choice forces poorly performing schools to do better. As a result of this choice, these schools would need to be keen and motivated to compete with other comprehensive schools.

Yet there are two sides to the argument. Surely if all pupils had to go to the local comprehensive there would be a fair spread of ability? In addition, there would be a better chance of developing a real community if these children all grew up attending the same school in the same area.

Since this would happen all over the country it would lead to schools doing better. You wouldn't have schools where no one was keen to go and which were the last choice for parents and pupils. Choice of school would not depend on how much you could pay for your house!

1 First read the opening paragraph. Pick out the main points of information and note them down as bullet points.

TRP p37

2 Now read the second and third paragraphs. Note down in bullet points the writer's main ideas in favour of parental choice.

3 List all the adjectives used in the second and third paragraphs.

4 Now read the fourth and fifth paragraphs. Note down in bullet points the writer's main ideas against parental choice.

5 List all the connectives used in the article.

6 The writer has used the simple structure of an introduction, followed by points in favour of choice (paragraphs 2 and 3) and then points against choice (paragraphs 4 and 5). Re-organise the ideas you listed as bullet points into a different structure – where you take each point in turn and look at it from both sides of the argument. Remember to link the paragraphs logically to make the sequence of your argument clear, using the list of connectives on page 79 to help you.

7 The writer hasn't finished this article. Write a suitable concluding paragraph for your version of the article, giving your own opinion on this issue.

TRP p38

ACTIVITY 7

1   Read this flyer about a public meeting in your town.

Say NO to radio masts!
Protect your environment!
Say NO to radio masts!

Britrail proposes to erect three 100ft radio masts in our neighbourhood in a bid to improve communications and safety on the rail network.

We strongly oppose this because:
  * **they are dangerous to health**
  * **they will be too close to homes and schools**
  * **they will be a blot on our landscape.**

Come to a meeting at St Michael's Church Hall on Wednesday 10 June at 7.30 p.m. to discuss this important issue.

The meeting will be attended by Mr J. Ferguson of the local council, Ms P. Smythe of Britrail and representatives of the Neighbourhood Preservation Committee.

Say NO to radio masts!
Protect your environment!

2   Imagine you attended the meeting about radio masts, which would be located near your school. Using the information in the flyer and your own ideas, write an article for the school magazine on the arguments put forward at the meeting.

 REMEMBER

Remember to:
→   organise your ideas
→   balance fact and opinion
→   give the arguments for and against
→   use suitable connectives to link your ideas.

TIMED WRITING   *(45 minutes)*

It is the turn of your class to present its concerns on an issue of school life to the whole school. As well as pupils, all the staff and governors will be present. The issue that most concerns your class is a proposal from the local education committee to reduce the money your school receives for music and drama in order to spend more money on IT facilities. Write the text of your speech presenting your argument against the plans of the local education committee. Copy and complete the planning grid below to help you plan your writing.

Suitable tone:

Points against the plans:

Possible points in favour of the plans:

Suitable emotive nouns and adjectives:

Suitable rhetorical questions:

Suitable connectives:

Ideas for the introduction:

Ideas for each paragraph:

Ideas for the conclusion:

C3 Advise

When you are writing to advise, you are trying to suggest what someone should do, how they should do it and why. You can use many of the same writing skills that you used in writing to persuade and writing to argue. In this unit, you will use these and other writing skills to create advice texts. You will also explore advice texts in the form of leaflets, letters and web pages.

You will focus on:

- thinking carefully about your audience and their needs
- considering all aspects of the situation to grab your readers' attention
- using emotive language
- using an appropriate style – impersonal or personal – depending on your audience.

↘ Using presentation devices in advice leaflets

Leaflets are one of the most common forms for writing to advise. They usually offer short, snappy advice. The most effective leaflets have the following features:

a presentation devices for maximum impact, for example headings, subheadings, bullet points, types of print, layout
b an understanding of the readers' concerns
c advice that addresses those concerns
d they may also give warnings.

ACTIVITY 1

1 Read the leaflet on page 90. Identify any of the features listed above that you can find.
2 Do you think the advice is effective? Give reasons for your answer.

BULLYING

What is bullying?

Bullying is when someone deliberately sets out to hurt, harass or intimidate someone else. Some of the ways bullying has been described are:

- ▶▶ calling you names
- ▶▶ telling lies to get you into trouble
- ▶▶ hitting, pinching, biting, pushing and shoving
- ▶▶ taking things away from you
- ▶▶ damaging your belongings
- ▶▶ stealing your money
- ▶▶ taking your friends away from you.

If you are being bullied:

- ▶▶ don't feel ashamed about it, it isn't your fault
- ▶▶ find someone you feel comfortable talking to and tell them what's happening
- ▶▶ try to remember things accurately by keeping a record of what has happened to you
- ▶▶ if you're being bullied at school, ask someone (such as a teacher) to find out about the school's policy on bullying as this might give you an idea of what you and your school can do about it.

If you know someone who's being bullied:

- ▶▶ don't ignore it
- ▶▶ let the person who's being bullied know that you are aware of what is going on
- ▶▶ encourage them to talk to someone.

Understanding readers' concerns

Readers usually respond best to advice that shows an understanding of problems or issues they can relate to. If this connection is made, the advice will be more successful.

ACTIVITY 2

Brainstorm ideas for a leaflet advising new pupils in your school of the advantages of attending the school homework club.

a   Pick out ideas that show you understand the problems pupils have in completing homework on time. Use your own experience and think about the times you were late with homework. What exactly caused those delays?

b   Find any links between the problems you have identified. List the problems that are linked together under various subheadings.

Keep your work for Activity 3.

The benefits of advice

Advice offers suggestions and/or guidance on how to deal with problems. There might be a clear solution to the problem, but good advice also explains the benefits of the solution to encourage readers to follow the advice.

ACTIVITY 3

1   Take each of the problems you identified in Activity 2 in turn and give an explanation of how the homework club can help to solve it. You could set out your ideas in a chart like this:

Problem	Homework club's solution

2   Using all the problems and solutions you have thought of, design an advice leaflet for the homework club. Use at least three presentation features in the design.

REMEMBER

Effective presentation features include:

→   headings
→   bullet points
→   a conclusion
→   layout

→   subheadings
→   an introduction
→   pictures and captions
→   types of print.

ACTIVITY 4

Many schools produce advice leaflets for pupils about healthy eating. To be effective, the leaflet would need to show clearly that pupils' difficulties in this area were understood.

1 Copy the chart below and list the difficulties in the first column. They might include those already listed, but add more from your own experience.

2 Now fill in the second column by writing two or three sentences that show understanding of the problem. One example has been done for you.

Difficulty	Show understanding	Advice
But I love sweets!	Everyone loves sweets – they taste delicious and make you feel good.	Try to replace one chocolate bar with a piece of fruit each day.

3 Now complete the chart by filling in advice to address each difficulty.

4 To be effective, the leaflet will need to be eye-catching enough to make pupils read to the end and benefit from the advice.

   a Think of one or more pictures that might be suitable for this leaflet. They could be amusing to grab attention, such as a fed-up pupil being told off by a teacher.

   b Decide where you would position the pictures on the leaflet. Would they be best at the top, the bottom or next to each piece of advice? Think carefully about where they will have the greatest effect.

Take warning

To make a powerful impact on issues that concern readers, many leaflets give warnings about possible dangers in our daily lives.

Think about the words you use when you are giving an urgent warning. Often the warning will only be one word with an exclamation mark, such as 'STOP!' or 'RUN!' Notice that these single-word warnings are verbs in the present tense and are called **imperatives**.

ACTIVITY 5

Copy and complete the chart below which lists issues that are often the basis of warning leaflets. Next to each one, write down some of the one-word present-tense verbs you might find on such leaflets. The first one has been done for you, but you may wish to add others.

Issue	One-word present-tense verbs
Smoking	*Stop. Quit.*
Lack of exercise	
Following school rules	
Talking to strangers	
Hygiene in the kitchen	
Surfing	

 TIMED WRITING *(30 minutes)*

Your school has a problem with unlicensed traders hanging around the school at lunchtime and after school. They try to sell illegal DVDs, videos and CDs to pupils.

Write a leaflet for pupils warning them of the dangers of buying from these traders. Indicate on your text where you might place appropriate pictures.

Copy and complete the planning grid on page 94 to help you.

continued ▶▶

93

Planning grid:

Introduction:

Message in each paragraph:

Message in the conclusion:

Powerful words and phrases:

Suitable presentation features to ensure leaflet is read:

Suitable pictures:

Advising with emotive language

Emotive language is not always appropriate if you want to offer advice that seems well balanced. However, it can be very useful if you want your audience to sit up with a jolt and take notice. The force of the words will bring home the message.

ACTIVITY 6

1 Copy and complete the following chart. It lists various dangers, with a rather mild warning about each one. Write a more forceful warning for each danger by replacing just one or two words with more emotive ones. The first one has been started for you.
2 Pictures are just as emotive as words. List what you would show in an illustration for each of the dangers.

Danger	Mild warning	Forceful warning	Illustration
Smoking	It can make your breath smell.	*It can make your breath stink.*	
Drugs	You might not be in full control of yourself.		
Road traffic	You might be involved in an accident.		
Credit cards	It is easy to finish up owing a lot of money.		
Dangerous sports	It is better to find a qualified instructor.		

TIMED WRITING *(30 minutes)*

Write a leaflet to be distributed to pupils in your school, which gives advice on solving problems by talking them through with a counsellor or a learning mentor. Remember that your audience is your fellow pupils and you must show that you understand their problems. Do not draw any pictures, but give very brief descriptions of what they would be and where they would be used. Copy and complete the following planning grid to help you.

The problems pupils face that would benefit from this solution:

Your experience of the same problems:

Advice suggesting solutions:

Suitable tone:

Suitable imperatives:

Introduction:

Message in each section:

Message in the conclusion:

Suitable pictures:

⤷ Improving an advice text from a website

The notes below are from a web page for teenagers on coping with exam pressure. As you can see, it is unfinished and in a rough draft form.

ACTIVITY 7

Copy out the notes and rewrite them, improving and completing the text. Aim to:

- expand the introduction to make it more interesting and to grab readers' attention
- add more advice to complete the lists of bullet points
- complete the unfinished sentences with useful advice
- add any more advice or information that you think would be helpful
- suggest any presentation devices you could use to make the text more interesting.

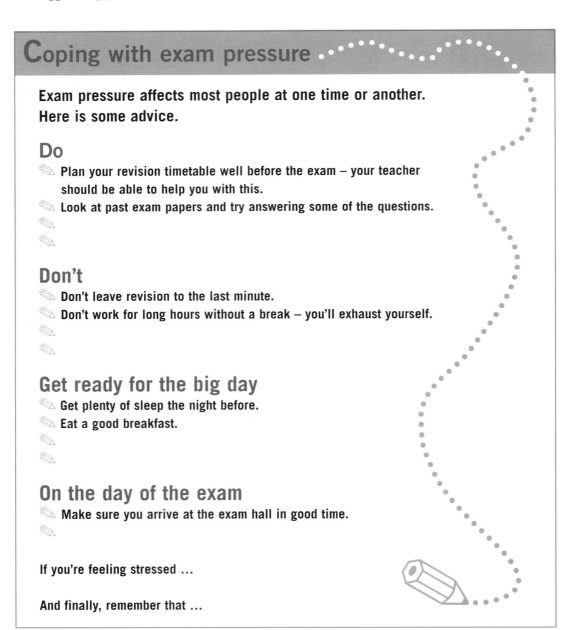

Coping with exam pressure

Exam pressure affects most people at one time or another. Here is some advice.

Do
- **Plan your revision timetable well before the exam – your teacher should be able to help you with this.**
- **Look at past exam papers and try answering some of the questions.**

Don't
- **Don't leave revision to the last minute.**
- **Don't work for long hours without a break – you'll exhaust yourself.**

Get ready for the big day
- **Get plenty of sleep the night before.**
- **Eat a good breakfast.**

On the day of the exam
- **Make sure you arrive at the exam hall in good time.**

If you're feeling stressed …

And finally, remember that …

⭲ Writing letters of advice

Not many people write letters regularly any more, but letters are an important form of writing which you need to know how to do.

Letters can certainly give advice. Just as with other kinds of texts, you need to think very carefully about the appropriate tone to use. You may well need a reassuring tone to convince readers that your advice is worth considering. This will involve choosing your words carefully.

ACTIVITY 8

1   Copy and complete the chart below. The words in the first column of the chart would contribute to an angry or challenging tone. Replace them with words that would contribute to a calming or reassuring tone. The first one has been done for you.

TRP
p40

Angry words	Calm words
fight	discuss
argue	
confront	
challenge	
instruct	
demand	

2   Now imagine that you are writing to a friend who is having problems with his father about when he does his homework. Plan the first two paragraphs of a letter in which you want to advise your friend in a reassuring tone by using words from the second column of the chart. Also consider:
   ● the age of your friend
   ● the appropriate balance between personal and impersonal styles
   ● the particular problems your friend is likely to have
   ● your own experience of similar problems
   ● the advice you want to offer.

3   Now write the first two paragraphs of the letter.

TIMED WRITING *(30 minutes)*

You are on the committee of a local cycling club that wants to produce some advice for new members on safe cycling around town. The committee has agreed that the information should go under four headings.

● Dress

● On the road

● Cycle maintenance

● Learning the ropes

Create an advice leaflet which will help new members of the club.

Copy and complete the following planning grid to help you.

Introduction:

Ideas for section on 'Dress':

Ideas for section 'On the road':

Ideas for section on 'Cycle maintenance':

Ideas for section on 'Learning the ropes':

Conclusion:

Reminders about writing to advise:

D Writing to analyse, review, comment

Writers may analyse an issue, event or text; they may review a play, film or computer game; or comment on a story in the news or another person's opinion. In this section, you will explore a range of non-fiction texts and use the skills that you learn to create your own pieces of writing.

Unit D1 will help you to write a balanced analysis that uses evidence and opinions. You will learn how to use a variety of connectives to link your ideas and how to organise your main points into paragraphs.

Unit D2 will help you to write an interesting and informative review of a film or play. You will learn how to use rhetorical devices to persuade your audience and how to use punctuation to make your meaning clear.

Unit D3 will help you to create a piece of writing in which you comment and give your own opinion on a topic. You will learn how to respond to a point of view, how to integrate annotations into your writing and how to justify your opinions.

Text	Audience	Purpose	Type of language	Source
Leader article about drug-taking.	Adults	● To analyse problems of drug-taking. ● To show the audience different opinions.	Formal language: ● makes it sound serious. ● assumes a certain level of education.	Broadsheet newspaper
Playstation game review.	Children, aged 10+	● To tell the audience about a new game. ● To judge and recommend it or not.	● Humour and wordplay make the audience laugh. ● Technical language assumes audience knowledge.	Playstation` website
Reader's letter on human cloning.	Adults, older children and teenagers	● To give an opinion. ● To be provocative.	● Informal language sounds like speech. ● Strong language makes audience react.	Tabloid newspaper

It's a good idea to collect texts that analyse, review and comment on topics that interest you. Look in magazines and newspapers and on the Internet to get a flavour of the range of styles and language used in these kinds of writing.

The chart shows examples of texts that analyse, review or comment. Copy it and fill it in for the texts you have collected. This will help you to think about how the texts are put together. The language in these texts can be formal or informal, technical, serious or humorous depending on the audience and purpose. Writing to analyse, review and comment usually involves taking something apart and examining it, and includes a judgement or opinion.

D1 Analyse

When you analyse something, you take it apart to see how it has been put together or you use evidence to support the points you want to make. In this unit, you will write an analysis using evidence.

You will focus on:

- using evidence and opinions to give a balanced view
- using connectives to link ideas
- linking paragraphs effectively.

 ## Getting the balance right

When you are writing an analysis, it is important to give more than one opinion or point of view and to give equal weight to both. Otherwise, your writing may become an argument for one particular view.

ACTIVITY 1

1   Read extracts A and B and the annotations below. Extract A puts forward one point of view, while B gives a more balanced view. Notice the ways that nouns, verbs, adverbs, adjectives and connectives are used.

This sentence makes an assertion; it is a strong statement.

The writer uses 'will' to show certainty.

This undermines the other point of view. 'Might' is a weaker verb and adds to the effect.

> Water is the most precious resource on earth: without it no life can survive. As global warming increases, we will have less rain. While some might welcome warmer summers, the harsh reality is that this will seriously affect crop farming and domestic water supplies.

This adverb strengthens the point. ——

 Extract A

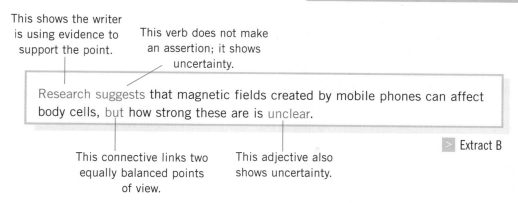

This shows the writer is using evidence to support the point.

This verb does not make an assertion; it shows uncertainty.

Research suggests that magnetic fields created by mobile phones can affect body cells, but how strong these are is unclear.

> Extract B

This connective links two equally balanced points of view.

This adjective also shows uncertainty.

2   Now look at extracts C and D below. Which one sets out one particular point of view and which one gives a more balanced analysis?

The fox is a pest and its population needs to be controlled. For farmers, uncontrolled growth in the fox population seriously damages their livelihood.

> Extract C

Opinion is divided as to the purposes of education. Some would argue that education should prepare young people for the skills they need in the world of work. Others believe that education should develop the ability to think critically, communicate clearly and access information.

> Extract D

ACTIVITY 2

You are about to read a balanced analysis of human cloning.

1   Before you read it, make a list of possible points for and against human cloning. Make a note of the kinds of people who might hold each particular view.

2   Read the text on page 102 and tick the points on your list which are mentioned in the text. Add to your list any that you did not predict.

3   What groups of people are mentioned in the text as holding particular points of view? What evidence is used?

Should humans be cloned?

Cloning facts

What is cloning?

When a cell is taken from one organism and used to create another organism, the new organism will be an exact copy. Dolly the sheep was created in this way.

Can humans be cloned?

There is no evidence that a human has been cloned, although a group called the Raelians have set up the company, Clonaid, to develop human cloning technology. They claim to have successfully cloned more than one human.

In the past few years, the topic of cloning has been in the news. It is a very controversial issue, with many opposing viewpoints. While some believe it is beneficial, others object for medical, religious or moral reasons.

One benefit of cloning is that people who are unable to have a baby naturally or who are too old to conceive could still have their own child. The cloned baby would actually be an exact copy of one parent.

Cloning could also allow organs to be cloned and used for transplant. Thousands of people die waiting for transplants, so this could save many lives. In addition, if the organs used in the transplant come from the same patient, this would reduce the risk of rejection by the body.

Nerves and spinal cords could be grown, giving quadriplegics the ability to walk again. Consider the case of actor Christopher Reeve, who played Superman. His spine was damaged in an accident and he is now in a wheelchair. He is a supporter of cloning research in the hope that one day he may be able to walk again.

One more benefit is that scientists may one day be able to reverse the aging process and as a result we could live longer.

However, there are also many reasons not to clone. A big concern is the possibility of abuse of this new technology. We may start by just experimenting and studying, but where will it lead? Will we go on to manufacturing human bodies for spare parts? No one can be sure where it will stop.

Another concern is the possibility of mutation. An abnormal baby could result from mutated genes. Some scientists are concerned that cloning would result in more abnormalities than natural conception. Experiments with animals suggest that this would be a very real danger in humans too.

In addition, cloning could cause emotional problems. A child cloned from one of its parents would be considered a delayed identical twin of that parent. Opponents argue that we cannot know how a person would react if they were an exact copy of an older individual.

Many religious groups, including some Roman Catholic and Muslim groups, also object to cloning. They argue that humans do not have the right to interfere with nature in this way.

There are many conflicting opinions on the subject of cloning. In spite of the potential benefits, there are equally many potential problems to be solved.

ACTIVITY 3

Before you start to write, plan the points you want to make in your analysis. Make sure you have roughly the same number of points for and against each of the main points of view. Aim for about three to five points for each.

Also consider what **evidence** and whose **opinions** you are going to use.

Look at the notes for the cloning article in the planning chart below. Copy and complete the chart.

Topic: Should humans be cloned?	
View 1: FOR	View 2: AGAINST
● *helps people who can't have children*	●
●	●
●	●
●	●
Evidence/opinions:	Evidence/opinions:
● *Christopher Reeve*	●
●	●

TIMED WRITING (10 minutes)

Choose one of the topics below. Make a note of the main points you could make and any **evidence** and **opinions** you could use. You could use a planning chart like the one above to help you plan your writing.

● Do children have enough freedom from adults these days?

● Are we becoming a nation of couch potatoes?

● Does television help to educate us or is it a waste of time?

● Should teenagers have to earn pocket money?

● Is advertising responsible for teenagers spending too much on designer goods?

● Is bullying a serious problem in today's schools?

● Should pupils have to wear school uniform?

● Is racism a serious issue in football?

● Space exploration – important scientific research or a waste of money?

↘ Linking your thinking

Writers use a range of language features to write a balanced analysis. You looked at some of them on pages 101–103. Now you will identify more language features and look in detail at how to link your ideas by using a variety of connectives.

ACTIVITY 4

1 Read the checklist below. It shows some techniques you could use to present a balanced analysis.

2 Look for examples of these techniques in the text about human cloning on page 102

FEATURES OF BALANCED ANALYSIS

- Use a variety of signal verbs to introduce evidence, for example:

  reports, points out, confirms, states, believes, agrees, disputes, denies, asserts.

- Use connectives to show cause and effect, for example:

  as a result, consequently, therefore, thus, this leads to, so, because, as.

- Use connectives to compare and contrast, for example:

  although, while, in spite of, however.

- Use impersonal language, for example:

  it is argued that, a widely held belief is that, it is commonly thought.

- Explain your evidence, for example by using verbs such as:

  shows, suggests, implies, indicates.

- Use rhetorical questions to involve or provoke the reader.

- Use repetition wisely to emphasise a point.

- Use tentative language such as modal verbs and conditionals to show uncertainty, for example:

  may, might, would, could, if, unless.

- Use language to signal different points of view, for example:

  some, others, one opinion is, opinion varies, opinion is divided.

- Invite readers to speculate, for example by using verbs such as:

  imagine, suppose, consider.

ACTIVITY 5

TRP
p50

1 Read the analysis of truancy below. The writer has planned this piece of writing well, but the sentences and writing style could be improved by using some of the features on the checklist on page 104.

2 Re-draft the text using the checklist. Some suggestions are given for the first paragraph to get you started.

Could link first and second sentences to show cause and effect, e.g. with 'and this has led to many articles in …'.

Should the parents of pupils who truant be sent to prison?

Pupil truancy is a big issue. It has been in the newspapers. People have had heated debates about it. It is a controversial issue. The government says parents are responsible. They should send their children to school. If they don't, they will go to prison. Other people don't agree. Social services say it punishes people who can't and won't work.

Could start with connective 'However' to introduce the other view as a contrast to the first. This would strengthen the point.

Could link this sentence to the one before with 'so'

The government is taking harsh action. It has introduced new measures to combat the problem of truancy. It has sent several parents to prison for failing to send their children to school. It says they must take their responsibilities as parents seriously and think about their children's education.

One mother with two daughters, living near Oxford, went to prison for several months. She said it was the best thing that happened to her. It gave her the shock she needed. Her two daughters don't truant any more. One of them said that she felt really bad that her mother was sent to prison for what she'd done.

Some people think that sending parents to prison is a harsh reaction. They say there are other ways of making parents ensure their children attend school. Social services say that these measures affect poorer people and groups such as single parents. They have more problems and difficulty in controlling their children. They need support (such as parenting skills courses). They don't need more stress. Their children need them at home. If the parents are sent to prison, their children will become even more wild.

The question of whether parents should be sent to prison for failing to ensure their children attend school regularly is a difficult one to answer. Parents who let their children take time off or who can't control their children need support. If all other efforts are made and they fail to work, prison is the only other option.

ACTIVITY 6

1 Complete the sentences below, using connectives from the chart. There may be more than one correct answer.

Connectives to show cause and effect	Connectives to compare and contrast
● as a result	● although
● therefore	● while
● so	● in spite of
● thus	● on the contrary
● consequently	● however
● as a consequence	● yet
● because	● whereas
● this leads to	● on the other hand
● this causes	● nevertheless

a .... many people believe that illegal drugs cause problems in society, others argue that alcohol is far more harmful.

b Some pupils are bullied in school and .... they may truant.

c .... fox hunting is considered a sport by many, others view it as cruel and inhumane.

d .... parental concerns, there is evidence that violence on television does not cause children to behave more aggressively.

e Space exploration costs billions of dollars, ... does it have any real benefits?

f Most people believe that global warming poses a threat to the future of our planet, ... they do nothing about it.

g Many young people today do not do enough physical activity or eat a healthy diet. .... obesity.

h .... government health warnings, people continue to smoke.

i School uniform can be seen as smart and practical, ... it can be seen as a way to destroy individuality.

j .... of over-protection by parents, today's teenagers are unskilled in making their own decisions.

2 Now work with a partner. Compare your answers and give reasons for your choices.

TIMED WRITING *(15 minutes)*

Now look back at the planning grid you completed on page 103. Write an opening paragraph for each topic using one or more of the connectives in the list above. To help you, you could look back at the opening paragraph of the article on cloning on page 102 to help you write your own opening paragraph.

↘ Linking the main points

A good writer helps readers by organising their ideas into main points and paragraphs. Each main point will be supported by smaller points.

A good writer also builds up a logical argument and shows the links between each paragraph, so that the whole piece of writing hangs together. Now you will look at some of the different ways of linking paragraphs.

ACTIVITY 7

1 Look at the annotated article 'Should humans be cloned?' on page 108. It shows how the analysis has been constructed and how the main points are linked.

2 Notice the way each paragraph is introduced and how it links to the previous one. Can you add any more ways of linking paragraphs to the ones listed in the box below?

Opening paragraph
- There are many different points of view
- ... many opposing viewpoints ...

Introducing examples
- Consider the case of ...
- One example would be ...

Concluding paragraph
- To summarise ...

Main body
- One argument is ...
- Another argument is ...
- One more view is ...
- In addition ...
- Moreover ...
- Also ...
- In contrast ...

TRP
p50

TIMED WRITING *(20 minutes)*

1 Read the extract below. It is the first paragraph of an analysis of the use of animals in medical experiments.

2 Write the next two paragraphs of this analysis. You could use some of the phrases in the article on page 108 and in the panel above to link your paragraphs together.

Should we experiment on animals?

The use of animals for medical experimentation is a very controversial issue. In the UK, one in every four animals, including cats, dogs, primates, rabbits, rats and mice suffer and die in laboratories in the name of research. On the other hand, such research has helped provide antibiotics and vaccines, insulin for diabetics, treatments for leukaemia, local and general anaesthetics, and has made possible advances in medical technology, such as blood transfusion, kidney dialysis and the heart-lung machine. So is it necessary or right to experiment on animals or is it unnecessary and cruel?

Should humans be cloned?

Introduction. First paragraph sets out main arguments for and against.

In the past few years, the topic of cloning has been in the news. It is a very controversial issue, with many opposing viewpoints. While some believe it is beneficial, others object for medical, religious or moral reasons.

These phrases show that a balanced view will be presented.

Signals the first main point.

One benefit of cloning is that parents who are unable to have a baby naturally or people who are too old to conceive could still have their own child. The cloned baby would actually be an exact copy of one parent.

Signals the second point.

Cloning could also allow organs to be cloned and used for transplant. Thousands of people die waiting for transplants, so this could save many lives. In addition, if the organs used in the transplant come from the same patient, this would reduce the risk of rejection by the body.

Introduces another closely related point.

Arguments for.

New point. For variety, writer uses a different way to introduce it.

Nerves and spinal cords could be grown, giving quadriplegics the ability to walk again. Consider the case of actor Christopher Reeve, who played Superman. His spine was damaged in an accident and he is now in a wheelchair. He is a supporter of cloning research in the hope that one day he may be able to walk again.

Supports the point being made in this paragraph.

One more benefit is that scientists may some day be able to reverse the aging process and as a result we could live longer.

Signals a change or contrast. The arguments against follow.

However, there are also many reasons not to clone. A big concern is the possibility of abuse of this new technology. We may start by just experimenting and studying, but where will it lead? Will we go on to manufacturing human bodies for spare parts? No one can be sure where it will stop.

New point

Another concern is the possibility of mutation. An abnormal baby could result from mutated genes. Some scientists are concerned that cloning would result in more abnormalities than natural conception. Experiments with animals suggest that this would be a very real danger in humans too.

In addition, cloning could also cause emotional problems. A child cloned from one of its parents would be considered a delayed identical twin of that parent. Opponents argue that we cannot know how a person would react if they were an exact copy of an older individual.

Arguments against.

Many religious groups, including some Roman Catholic and Muslim groups, also object to cloning. They argue that humans do not have the right to interfere with nature in this way.

Final paragraph sums up without favouring one viewpoint or the other.

There are many conflicting opinions on the subject of cloning. In spite of the potential benefits, there are equally many potential problems to be solved.

TIMED WRITING *(45 minutes)*

Swanbury School Council

Should pupils be allowed to have mobile phones in school?

The School Council is to discuss this issue at the next meeting.

Pupil class representatives should attend. All other pupils welcome.

Write a speech from the point of view of a Year 9 pupil to give at the School Council meeting, analysing what you think are the advantages and disadvantages of pupils bringing mobile phones to school. Use a grid like the one below to help you plan your ideas.

Advantages:

Disadvantages:

Words / phrases you could use:

 REMEMBER

→ Plan your writing and make sure you have enough points to make.

→ Plan some of the words and phrases you will use.

→ Include words and phrases that indicate a balanced analysis.

→ Use a variety of connectives to link your thinking.

→ Write in paragraphs and choose phrases to link paragraphs clearly.

1 Work with a partner. Read your partner's text and identify the features your partner has used.

2 Are the features your partner has used effective? Tell your partner two positive aspects about their writing and make two suggestions for how they might improve it.

D2 Review

When you review something, you evaluate its strengths and weaknesses. In this unit, you will read reviews of adventure holidays, explore different review texts and write your own film review.

You will focus on:

- choosing the right level of formality for the audience and purpose
- using rhetorical devices to persuade your audience
- using a range of punctuation to make your meaning clear.

↘ Degrees of formality

A good writer carefully chooses the level of formality of vocabulary and grammar to suit the audience and purpose. When writing a review, you need to think about your audience and purpose and then decide whether to use formal or informal language, or a mixture of both. You should also engage your audience and tell them about the positive and negative aspects of whatever you are reviewing.

ACTIVITY 1

1 Look at the continuum, which shows words of similar meaning but with differing degrees of formality.

Formal ⟶	**Informal** ⟶	**Colloquial / slang**
elated	happy	over the moon

2 Read the words below and group them together in sets of three with similar meanings. Place each set of three on a continuum.

● fatigued	● get it	● done in	● tired	● recruit
● understand	● escape	● do a runner	● comprehend	● indirect
● abscond	● take on	● circuitous	● roundabout	● hire

3 Do you use any different slang terms for any of the words above? What are they?

ACTIVITY 2

1 Study these lists of the features of formal and informal texts.
2 Read the two extracts from reviews on activity holidays on pages 111 and 112 and look for examples of formal and informal language. Use the checklists to help you.
   a What is the audience and purpose of each extract?
   b How is the degree of formality of the language linked to the audience and purpose?

FEATURES OF FORMAL TEXTS

Formal texts tend to have more:
abstract nouns, for example *'life'*, *'ignorance'*.
non-human subjects of sentences, for example *'The sun is the only source of light and heat in the universe.'*
passive verb forms, for example *'Ford cars are manufactured in Dagenham.'*
subordinate clauses, for example *'Even when not at war, submarines are dangerous.'*
impersonal tone, for example, be written in third person, be distant from audience.

FEATURES OF INFORMAL TEXTS

Informal texts tend to have more:
concrete nouns, for example *'streets'*, *'people'*.
human subjects of sentences, for example *'Young people don't have enough independence these days.'*
active verb forms, for example *'The band toured Europe last summer.'*
co-ordinating clauses, for example *'You can travel by bus, but it is quicker by train.'*
personal tone, for example, may address audience directly, be written in first person, use *'fillers'* such as *As I said before* or modifiers such as *really*, or include personal anecdotes.

Adventure Travel (for Wimps)

Flying, diving and surfing sound fun but scary? I did all three on the Hawaiian island of Oahu, no nerves of steel required. And you don't have to spend big bucks getting there. Face your fears and have some fun!

Diving

Scuba diving sounds awesome – being able to breathe underwater and see all the different fishes swimming right by you like you were one of them. But you have to take a bunch of training courses and get certified before you can go. Enter snuba – the perfect happy medium where you can dive 25 feet under but instead of carrying the oxygen on your back, you're attached by a tube to a little float on the surface that holds your tank. Much less scary, no certification needed. After just a quick equipment orientation in the pool, we headed out on the boat.

I strapped on my gear – mouthpiece, face mask and weight belt to help me sink to the ocean bottom. Then the instructor took me into the water and we started to descend. And that's when I started to panic. I was breathing heavily, and totally paranoid about making my ears pop at all the right times to accommodate for the extra pressure underwater. I quickly decided that I had sufficiently been there and done that, and headed back to the surface. (Hey, I said I was a wimp!) I'll try it again sometime, but for now I'm just pretty impressed with myself for taking the plunge at all.

Wanna do it?

Most big dive spots now offer snuba as well as snorkelling and scuba.

> From *seventeen.com online* magazine

The Truth about Mount Kinabalu

By Jocasta Webb

It was with some trepidation that I set off in an overcrowded people carrier from Kota Kinabalu to the Kinabalu National Park to climb the highest mountain in South-east Asia. Thus far, my mountaineering experience had been confined to Britain, and never higher than 1400 m. Less than half an hour from the capital, the stegosaurus-backed Mount Kinabalu, standing at an impressive 4095.2 m, came into view, promising a tropical adventure.

Arriving at the park headquarters, while organising accommodation, climbing permits and the compulsory booking of a guide for the climb, it struck me how the mountain climb was played down. The map of the summit trail was a poor quality photocopy of a rough hand-drawing, most of which was illegible. No questions were asked concerning experience or fitness, and no advice was offered regarding what precautionary items to take. In addition, no detailed weather forecast seemed to be available. At that point, taking a guide appeared somewhat superfluous. Persistent rain and all-enveloping cloud left me with thoughts of North Wales. Maybe this was not the tropical adventure I was hoping for after all.

> From *The Guardian online*

TIMED WRITING   (20 minutes)

Rewrite the first article for a teenage audience, changing the vocabulary and sentence structure to make it less formal.

Persuading your audience: rhetorical devices

In reviews, writers will give the audience some facts about whatever they are reviewing. They will also describe what they think are its negative and positive aspects or its strengths and weaknesses. Writers may recommend whatever they are reviewing or they may not. To do this, writers sometimes use language to persuade their audience to their point of view. Rhetorical devices help them to do this.

TRP
p52

ACTIVITY 3

1 Read the review below and the two on page 114 and answer the following questions.
   a What is being reviewed?
   b Who is the audience?
   c What is the purpose of the review?
   d Does the writer like or dislike the item being reviewed?
   e How formal or informal is the language?
   f How does the degree of formality of the language relate to the audience and purpose?

Title: Dinomania: Things to do with Dinosaurs
Authors: Mick Manning and Brita Granstrom
Publisher: Watts
Price: £ 9.99
Age: 5–10
Reviewer: Lindsey Fraser

A model of cross-curricular publishing, this book is full of information, but also of dinosaur-related activities, from dressing up, to making an active volcano (to mark the dinosaurs' extinction), to making edible dinosaur droppings, to filming a video, the script of which David Attenborough would be proud. Dinosaurs exert an uncanny hold over most children and this imaginatively constructed blend is ideal. Whether you are a teacher looking for a fresh perspective on a well-worn topic, or a parent hoping to have your child placed in their next fancy dress competition, this is a splendid investment.

> From *The Guardian Education Book of the Week Reviews Supplement*

Overall: 5 Gameplay: 4 Graphics: 5 Sound: 4

General/summary: Sony's latest F1 effort has come together well, with good, solid gameplay and graphics. Playing on it is very enjoyable and entertaining (even on boring circuits), especially after you've set up the car yourself! It is a good game for anyone to pick up and play, with several levels of difficulty.

Gameplay: The cars' handling is realistic, with the Ferraris having a significant edge over the Minardis. With driving aids on, it is relatively easy, but turn off ABS, traction control and select manual gears and the game is taken into a whole new dimension. The other cars' AI is much better than in previous games – they make mistakes and can even put themselves out! However, the AI cars have an advantage, though hairpins and starts are boring with the AI cars all starting at the same time. Also, the cars' front wings fall off when you hit them in the rear and the performance levels aren't quite right.

Graphics: Graphics are superb on this game. The cars look ultra-realistic. What else can I say?

Sound: The cars sound fantastic, with different engines producing different sounds. Murray and Martin also sound better (although you can hear the phrasing stuck together) than in previous games.

> From www.videogamesreview.com

Watch this

Unconditional Love
9pm, ITV 1
This one-off, expertly-paced, nerve-jangling child kidnap drama from *Murder in Mind* director Ferdy Fairfax will do the waning and, literally, waxing reputations of its leads, the one-and-only Robson Green and Sarah Parish, no harm at all. Green and the *Cutting It* star play the doting parents of little Max Gregg, who goes missing during his fourth birthday party. 'Ninety-nine times out of 100, they turn up', reasons the sadly little-seen Peter Capaldi, who plays the weary investigating detective, just before Max's disappearance turns into every parent's nightmare.

> From *The Guardian*

2   Choose one of the reviews and find examples of the language features listed in the chart opposite. Copy the chart and complete it with the examples you have found.

Review of		
Language feature	**Many/few**	**Example**
Adjectives		
Technical/specialist vocabulary		
Short sentences		
Complex sentences		
Formal language		
Informal language		
Repetition		
Rhetorical questions		
Metaphors or similes		
Word play (e.g. puns, alliteration, jokes)		
Any other features you have noticed		

3 Compare your analysis with those of pupils who have looked at the other reviews.
   a What similarities or differences do you notice?
   b Can you generalise about typical features of a review?

Using adjectives

One way of persuading your audience is by choosing adjectives carefully. Some adjectives don't tell us very much at all (such as 'nice', 'good') and should be avoided. Think about precisely what you want to say to persuade your audience. Choose an adjective – either formal or informal as appropriate – that will do the job well.

ACTIVITY 4

1 Working with a partner, brainstorm some alternatives to the words 'good' and 'bad'.
2 Look at this list of formal adjectives, arranged in positive and negative pairs, which could be used in the review of a film. Think of more adjectives to add to the list. You could use a dictionary or thesaurus to help you.

Aspect of the film	Positive	Negative
The plot	gripping	predictable
The graphics	realistic	unrealistic
The scenery	stunning	dull
The acting	convincing	unconvincing
The story	engaging	unbelievable

3 To be really original, make up your own adjectives, especially if you want to create an informal tone. Here are two ways that you can create new adjectives.

a Look at these examples from 'Watch this' on page 114:

Little-seen detective	= adjective + verb	(we don't see him very much)

Expertly-paced drama	= adverb + verb	(the pace is expertly achieved)

Nerve-jangling drama	= noun + verb	(the drama is really gripping)

Remember that when you make up your own adjectives they can be positive or negative.

b The adjective 'ultra-realistic' is used in the video game review on page 114. You can also put other prefixes in front of an adjective in a similar way. For example:

hyper-	mega-	super-

This kind of adjective helps to intensify the meaning.

4 Make up some adjectives of your own to describe:
- a horror movie
- a comedy
- a wildlife documentary
- a detective story
- a computer game
- a romance.

5 Now make sentences using your adjectives. For example:

> This hyper-overrated computer game won't exactly have you gripping your console.

⬎ Punctuating to make a point

Good writers use punctuation to make their meaning clear, emphasise a point or show their attitude, for example to show humour. Now you will look at how writers use commas, dashes and brackets.

ACTIVITY 5

1 Before reading the review of the film The Fellowship of the Ring opposite, discuss what you know about the film or the book. Predict five things you think the reviewer will say.

2 Now read the review. Make a list of the positive and negative points the writer makes.

3 Overall, does the writer recommend the film?

'Precious' Metal

By Tim Curphey

Peter Jackson's movie is a triumph. A bloodily enthusiastic, visually stunning cinematic rendition of Tolkien's legendary book. In the creation of this film Jackson's true victory lies in his devotion to the honesty and sincerity of a story, so soaked in mysticism and chain-mail bravado that, if taken on by a less recognised (or more Hollywoodised) director, could easily have slipped into something ridiculous.

Our entrance into Middle Earth begins with a dark and violent prologue that sets us straight on the origins of the ring, its evil creator Sauron and the awesome power that it wields. (As a precursor, this is CG (computer graphics) at its most monumental, raising expectations high for what is to follow ...) Yet what immediately follows seems the only hurdle Jackson doesn't quite clear in his two-and-a-half-hour depiction; for Hobbiton, where our hero Frodo (Elijah Wood) and his wizard mentor/pal Gandalf the Grey (Ian McKellen) reside, feels and looks, with its Morris Men-festooned party atmosphere and its vertically challenged, weed-smoking, numbskull natives, ridiculously sweet. Could our hero really be from these 'ere parts? Astonishingly, he is ...

This said, Hobbiton is a sturdy enough foundation for Jackson to launch his narrative from, and so he does as Bilbo (Ian Holm), Frodo's cantankerous old uncle and current possessor of the ring, sets out on an OAP's jaunt around Middle Earth (no bus pass required), leaving Frodo with the ring and in a world of danger. For the ring's creator wants it back to use for domination of Middle Earth. In order to save his much-loved world, Frodo is informed that he must (and can only) destroy the ring in the fires in which it was forged – Sauron's Mount Doom. For this colossal endeavour Frodo joins a consortium of Middle Earth dwellers – an elf, a dwarf, two humans, a wizard and three other hobbits – to form The Fellowship, a.k.a. Middle Earth's version of the SAS, and begins the quest for their world's salvation.

It is at this point in the film – when the quest is truly embraced – that Jackson's epic propels itself into the next league of cinema. Jackson has a fascination with grunge and gore (as his earlier works of *Bad Taste* and *Brain Dead* lay testament to) and he pulls no punches here as Frodo's tribe are set upon by all manner of horrors – cow-pat-faced orcs, savage Uruk Hai warriors (picture WWF wrestlers from hell) and in the mines of Moria, not one but three gargantuan creatures. The evil in this film is truly palpable.

Much of the movie's power is in its design; for this, Jackson brought in Tolkien book illustrators, Alan Lee and John Howe, who inspired a stunning spectrum of environments for the celluloid: majestic landscapes, ethereal towers and creepy caverns all interlock with ease, bringing Tolkien's fantastic grand design to life.

continued ▸▸

Wonderful performances lie at the heart of the film: Wood's pint-sized hero is fabulous – wide-eyed, naive and fallible but with a will of iron. His allies, specifically Bloom's dainty yet aggressive peroxide-blonde elf, Legolas and Sean Bean's conflicted, Shakespearean Boromir are a treat to watch. And Christopher Lee's wizard Saruman is as wicked a role as he has ever played.

The Fellowship of the Ring is a darkly magnificent film with a strong vision. Jackson, like his movie's characters, has taken up a mission, to transform modern epic cinema and in this he has valiantly succeeded. As one character says in the film, 'Even the smallest person can change the shape of the future.' How true! Mr Jackson, you have done us proud.

Using commas in complex sentences

ACTIVITY 6

1   Match the main clauses and the subordinate clauses below to make three complex sentences.

Main clause
I would recommend this horror film
The exhibition was fairly interesting
Harrison Ford … is excellent.

Subordinate clause
although it was very crowded.
who plays the main character
if you have a strong stomach.

Rules for punctuation

Main clause + subordinate clause = no comma, for example:

> *The action begins as soon as the opening credits roll.*

Subordinate clause + main clause = a comma after subordinate clause, for example:

> *Unless you are a real romantic, you will loathe this film.*

Embedded clause (a subordinate clause in the middle of the main clause) = a comma either side of the subordinate clause, for example:

> *Michael DeWitt, whose acting abilities are somewhat limited, is totally unbelievable as a successful doctor.*

TRP
p52

2   Place commas where they are needed in the sentences in Question 1 above.

Using brackets and dashes

ACTIVITY 7

Brackets and dashes can be used to punctuate text, instead of, or as well as, using a subordinate clause, to make writing sound more informal.

Look at these sentences from the review on page 117–118, which show how the writers have used brackets and dashes.

● Dashes can be used to insert details.

> For this colossal endeavour Frodo joins a consortium of Middle Earth dwellers – an elf, a dwarf, two humans, a wizard and three other hobbits – to form The Fellowship

● Brackets can be used to talk directly to the reader.

> Jackson has a fascination with grunge and gore (as his earlier works of *Bad Taste* and *Brain Dead* lay testament to)

● Brackets and dashes can be used to emphasise the point being made.

> ... so soaked in mysticism and chain-mail bravado that, if taken on by a less recognised (or more Hollywoodised) director, could easily have slipped into something ridiculous.

● Dashes are used to expand and emphasise the first point.

> It is at this point in the film – when the quest is truly embraced – that Jackson's epic propels itself into the next league of cinema.

● Brackets and dashes can also be used to give a personal view or make a humorous comment.

> ... savage Uruk Hai warriors (picture WWF wrestlers from hell)

 TIMED WRITING   *(15 minutes)*

Choose a book, film, game or product to review. Write three or four sentences about it using brackets and dashes to do one or more of the following:
● add more information
● talk to the reader
● add a personal comment
● emphasise the main point.

TIMED WRITING *(45 minutes)*

Westside School Magazine

Calling all pupils!

We need film and play reviews for the next issue of the school magazine.

Write a review of a film or play you have seen for the school magazine from the point of view of a Year 9 pupil. It could be about a film version or live production of the Shakespeare play you are studying. Use a grid like the one below to plan your review.

Possible areas for review	Positive points	Negative points
Acting		
Costume		
Make up		
Effects		
Scenery		
Location		
Sound		
Overall view		Words/phrases you could use

! REMEMBER

→ Plan your review and decide on the positive and negative points you want to make.

→ Overall, will your review be positive or negative?

→ Decide how formal or informal your language will be.

→ Choose some rhetorical devices to persuade your audience.

→ Use a variety of punctuation to make your meaning clear.

1 Work with a partner. Read your partner's text and identify the features he/she has used.

2 Are the features your partner has used effective? Tell your partner two positive aspects about their writing and make two suggestions for how they might improve it.

D3 Comment

When you comment on something, you give a considered opinion based on available evidence and opinions. Written commentary is typically found in newspaper editorials, the main body of news reports, letters to newspaper editors, and chat and debate websites. In this unit, you will write comments giving your opinions.

You will focus on:

- understanding the writer's viewpoint
- giving evidence to justify your opinions
- using speech marks to integrate quotation into your writing
- showing you have an informed opinion.

↘ Understanding the writer's viewpoint

Writers do not always directly state their point of view by saying, for example, 'I believe' or 'I think'. Sometimes they use more subtle or indirect ways of putting their view across. Now you will take on the role of detective and spot how writers do this.

ACTIVITY 1

1 Do you think that rap music is responsible for the increase in gun-related crime in the UK? Discuss your views with a partner.
2 Read the newspaper article on page 122 about whether hip-hop music is responsible for the increase in gun culture and violent crime. What is the writer's opinion?
3 Read the annotations around the article. How does the writer comment on this issue?
4 Pick out some words, phrases and sentences that show the writer's opinion.
5 Apart from hip-hop, what other causes of the growth of gun culture are given in the text?
6 What do you think are the reasons for the growth of gun culture? Look at the following list of possibilities.

- Rap music glamorises guns and incites violence. Radio stations which play rap music encourage violence.

- The police are racist and don't care when the victims and perpetrators of violent crimes are black.

- Parents don't control their children's behaviour.

- Schools don't educate young people about the dangers of guns.

- Criminals know that witnesses won't talk to the police.

- The government doesn't do enough to clamp down on illegal guns.

- The illegal gun trade means that guns are too easily available.

- The law doesn't give sentences that are harsh enough.

continued ▶▶

- The media give a distorted picture by over-reporting gun crimes.
- Unemployment and poverty cause those who suffer to resort to crime.

a Rank the reasons from 1 for most important to 10 for least important.

b Share your views with a partner.

TRP
p53

Why hip-hop must take its share of blame for spread of violence among teenagers

By Caroline Sullivan

Does hip-hop glamorise gun culture? It depends who you ask. Guns have been part of the baggage of hip-hop since 1988, when Los Angeles' NWA released what was arguably the first gangsta-rap album, Straight Outta Compton.

Its robust depiction of violence turned what had been a party genre on its head – and opened it up to slackerly white teenagers who had until then seen it as a black thing.

Two threads emerged from the ensuing debate, generating the clichés that persist to this day. On one hand, NWA claimed their songs amounted to simple reportage – the 'we're just reflecting real life' defence. Others, from the FBI to the black rights organisation NAACP, detected a shocking amorality.

> This word suggests the writer does not believe what NWA say.

Fifteen years later, neither side has given an inch. Kim Howells accuses 'hateful lyrics' of inciting violence, while the biggest British rap/garage act, So Solid Crew argue that gun culture is the by-product of escalating poverty, and they can't be blamed if they are caught up in it on their south London estates.

Does anyone detect a get-out clause along the same lines as the National Rifle Association slogan 'Guns don't kill people. People kill people'?

> The writer uses sarcasm to suggest that So Solid Crew are making excuses.

But the situation is more complex than it was in the days of NWA and Snoop Dogg (the former spliff-smoking scourge who has evolved into a thirty-something businessman with his own clothing range). Some insist that envious 'haters' make guns a necessity.

So Solid member Ashley 'Asher D' Walters cited self-defence when he was convicted of possession a year ago, and he's not the only UK urban denizen to be steeped in the gang-based way of seeing things. (That said, last year's Brit Awards incident in which a member of Westlife offered to fight the whole Crew ripped an embarrassing hole in their tough image, and months of negative publicity have taken much of the wind out of their sails.)

> The writer makes an assertion to make her opinion look like fact.

What it boils down to is that teenage boys are impressionable and always will be. Just reflect that the Sex Pistols once persuaded fans that spitting at each other was fantastically cool.

> Evidence is provided of how fans of the Sex Pistols copied their bad behaviour.

It takes several leaps of the imagination to apply the same logic to guns, but it happens. So no, hip-hop can't claim to be entirely innocent here.

> From *The Guardian*

TIMED WRITING *(20 minutes)*

Now write two paragraphs to support your view on the causes of the growth of gun culture. Use some of the techniques used by the writer of the article on page 122. Remember to avoid using overdone words like 'I believe' or 'I think'.

↘ Backing up your point of view

To make your comments more convincing, you need to support them. You can do this by:

- using evidence from facts and figures
- quoting experts' and other people's opinions
- giving examples from your own knowledge and experience.

ACTIVITY 2

1 Read the comments about gun culture in the UK in the following three extracts below and on page 124. Then sum up the main point of view in each extract and note down the evidence given to support it. Copy and complete a chart like the one below.

Viewpoint	Evidence (e.g. facts, personal experience, expert opinion)
A *Children are getting into trouble because their parents don't know what they're doing.*	*Opinion/personal experience*
B	
C	

Extract A quotes Ivor Etienne, discussing rising gun crime on a Saturday lunchtime phone-in on Choice FM, an urban radio station based in South London.

> We're not looking after our young children and teaching them the proper values ... It's a family issue. Some parents aren't asking their children where they've been and who they're seeing until the alarm bells start ringing. If kids want to get into a clique, it's easy to drift in.

> From *The Observer*

Extract B quotes Elaine Sihera, magazine publisher, commentator and founder of the British Diversity Awards and the Windrush Achievement Awards.

> The media never report 'white-on-white' crime ... Guns are carried by all types of people, white and black, but the reporting creates a perception that a higher proportion of black people carry guns.

> From *The Observer*

Extract C quotes Lucy Cope, Chair of Southwark Mothers Against Guns; her son Damian, 22, was fatally shot in central London in July 2002 by a man he named before his death as a black gang member; the suspect has since fled the country.

> There should be a minimum sentence of five years for possessing a handgun and a ban on imitation guns – which can be bought for £25 and modified to fire live bullets. People are saying that years down the line this country will be like the Bronx. They're wrong – it's months down the line.

> From *The Observer*

2   Notice some of the ways the speakers have cited evidence to support their comments, for example: 'reporting creates' and 'people are saying'.

The chart below gives you some ideas of whose opinions you could use to give evidence and some verbs you could use to introduce them. Add some more ideas of your own.

Source	Verbs to introduce them
● millions of people	● argue
● most people	● show
● experts	● suggest
● scientists	● agree
● experiments	● disagree
● parents	● prove
● responsible adults	● say
● research	● imply
● public opinion	● point out
● the general public	● think

 TIMED WRITING   *(15 minutes)*

Now write some sentences of your own to practise citing evidence, for example:
Most parents say they act responsibly and bring their children up to behave well.
The general public agrees that something must be done to stop the rise in gun-related crime.

Using quotations

When commenting, writers will often refer to another opinion to either support or counter it. If they want to use the exact words of someone else, writers must put speech marks around the words to show that they are a quotation, taken from somewhere else. Quotations are often short – just a few words or a phrase – when used in comments. Writers sometimes use a quotation to show how ridiculous they consider the opinion to be.

ACTIVITY 3

1   Look at the following three ways in which writers can show that they are about to use a quotation. They can:

●   use a signal phrase, such as 'says that', 'describes', 'blames' or 'suggests that', for example:

> Kim Howell accuses 'hateful lyrics' of inciting violence.

●   make it part of their sentence, for example:

> Does anyone detect a get-out clause along the same lines as the National Rifle Association slogan 'Guns don't kill people, people kill people'?

●   introduce the quotation with a colon or dash, for example:

> On one hand, NWA claimed their songs amounted to simple reportage – the 'we're just reflecting real life' defence.

2   Now experiment with the quotation 'hip-hop can't claim to be entirely innocent here' from the article on page 122. Argue against the writer's point, using the quotation in each of the ways given above.

 TIMED WRITING   *(20 minutes)*

1   Read the views below. Do you agree or disagree with each of them?
  a   While I agree that giving money to homeless people is pointless, it is not for the reason people might assume. The most effective way of getting homeless people off the streets is to donate your money to one of the charities that provide shelter, support for job hunting and help in securing accommodation.
  b   Young people are too easily manipulated by advertising. They only have to see the latest commercial for a particular brand of trainers and they are pestering their parents to buy them. Advertisers use this and deliberately direct their campaigns at teenagers.
2   Select a phrase from each view to quote in your response.
3   Write a comment of three to four sentences in response to each view.

↘ Informed opinion

When you comment on something it strengthens your own case if you show that you have made an informed opinion. If you show that you know what the opposing viewpoint is, destroy it and then present stronger points to support your own point of view, it will have more impact. You can also strengthen your case by making it seem more rational or logical than the opposing case. This is called using counter-argument.

The game below helps you to practise this skill.

The opposing views game

Before you play the game, read the statements and the chart of words and phrases below.

- Boys are more aggressive than girls.
- We don't respect old people in our society today.
- Young people's social skills are suffering because they spend too much time playing computer games.
- Education is the key to getting a well-paid job.
- Families don't spend enough time together these days.

Useful words and phrases for countering other points of view		
Phrases to introduce the opposing view	Connectives to signal an opposing point of view	Adverbs and phrases to make your view seem more rational or logical
1 While I agree that …	1 But	1 Obviously
2 It's true (to some extent) that …	2 However	2 Naturally
3 It might seem that …	3 On the other hand	3 Surely
4 Although …	4 Still	4 Clearly
5 … has a point in that …	5 Nevertheless	5 Of course
6 Some would argue that …	6 Despite this	6 No-one would doubt that …

To play this game you need to divide into groups of four. Each group will need a dice.

1 Each group of four divides into two pairs. One pair will be A and the other, B.
2 Pair A selects a statement from the list and reads it out to pair B.
3 Pair B quickly decides which aspect of the statement they agree with (their argument) and the main point against (their counter-argument).
4 Pair B throws the dice to select a phrase, which will introduce their argument, from the first column in the chart. They then say the first part of their argument aloud.
5 Then pair B repeats this procedure with words from the second and third columns to construct their counter-argument.
6 Pair A then repeats the procedure and they throw the dice to select words from each column to reply to the argument put forward by pair B.

7 Play the game again. This time with pair
B going first.

Here is an example, using the first statement in
the list, to help you get started.

> *It might seem that* boys are more aggressive than
> girls because boys are often in the news for
> committing violent crimes and we think of gangs
> as being mostly boys.
> *However*, girls can be as aggressive as boys.
> Nowadays there are many girl gangs and girl-
> fights in the playground. Girls are also
> committing violent crimes.
> *Obviously* not all boys are aggressive and not all
> girls are passive. Both are equally capable of
> both types of behaviour.

TIMED WRITING *(45 minutes)*

The following extract expresses a view that adults commonly have of young people.
This view is not new – the ancient Greeks had a similar opinion about young people!

> The trouble with young people today is that they don't know how to behave.
> They have no sense of responsibility. You only have to look at the increase in
> poor behaviour, school truanting and worsening exam results to see that this is
> true. The general public has to tolerate rudeness in the streets, in shops and
> on buses. And do you ever see a young person give up their seat for an elderly,
> pregnant or disabled person nowadays? It was different in my time …

As a young person, how do you respond to this comment? Use the bullet points below
to plan your comments.

● Briefly say what the issue is.

● Decide on your main point.

● Give two or three pieces of evidence for your view.

● Use quotations from the extract above or from any other sources in your argument.
  Decide on the words and phrases you will use to introduce them.

● Summarise with a strong final comment.

1 Work with a partner. Read your partner's text and identify the features your partner
  has used.

2 Are the features your partner has used effective? Tell your partner two positive aspects
  about their writing and make two suggestions for how they might improve it.

E Preparing for the Key Stage 3 writing tests

At the end of Year 9 you will take the Key Stage 3 National Curriculum English tests. Three areas are tested: reading, writing and Shakespeare. These tests will help you and your teacher see how much progress you have made since you took the Key Stage 2 English test at the end of Year 6. You may have measured your progress in the optional tests for Years 7 and 8, and you will find that the Year 9 tests are similar in many ways.

So far this book has focused on the skills you need to improve your writing and has provided plenty of practice to help you prepare for the writing test. This section focuses on the test papers themselves and:

- explains what is involved in the writing tests
- provides practice tests so that you become more familiar with the kinds of tasks that you will meet in the tests.

The writing tasks

There are two writing tasks in the writing test – a longer one and a shorter one. The longer writing task is worth 30 marks and you are allowed 45 minutes for it, including 15 minutes of planning and preparation. The shorter task is worth 20 marks and you are allowed 30 minutes for it. Of course, you will need to plan the shorter task carefully too, but no suggested time is given for planning and preparation.

The number of marks allocated and the time allowed for each writing task gives you a good idea about the amount you are expected to write in each case. Your response to the longer writing task is expected to be fairly detailed and wide-ranging, while your response to the shorter writing task will be brief and more focused.

The skills for each task

Your writing responses are marked for a number of different qualities. The longer and shorter tasks are marked in a slightly different way, although they test the same range of writing skills. The reason for marking the two tasks differently is that they require you to do different things.

- In the longer writing task, you will be able to show how you shape individual sentences and then organise them into a whole text, and how you choose to use and link paragraphs within an overall structure.
- In the shorter writing task, how you use sentence structures within paragraghs will be important.
- You are also more able to concentrate on the accuracy of your spelling in a shorter piece of writing, so spelling is assessed in the shorter task.

⇘ The planning time

You should use about 15 minutes of the time allocated for the longer writing task for planning and preparation. The paper contains a planning frame to help you gather together and organise your ideas, and to help you think about the best ways of expressing them. You will find this planning frame extremely helpful and if you use it, the piece of writing you produce is likely to be much better than if you simply start writing straight away. This will apply particularly to the marks available for structure and organisation.

In the actual writing test, you are not provided with a planning frame for the shorter writing task. However, you should still use 5 or 6 minutes to make brief notes in the answer booklet on the content and structure of your answer. In order to help you develop your planning skills, the shorter practice tasks in this book include planning frames, as well as some advice on each particular task.

Giving the best responses

For the best chance of getting high marks it is important that you:

- **do exactly what you are asked.** For example, if you are asked to write a speech, you will get no marks for writing a letter
- **answer the question that is asked.** Make sure that you include only material that answers the question. For example, the question will never ask you to include pictures, so do not waste your time drawing them
- **respond to all the prompts** (such as bullet points), if any are given
- **complete both tasks in the time allowed.** Plan your time carefully.

⇘ Marks

Your teacher has mark schemes for the practice tests in this book. Using these mark schemes, your teacher will be able to assess your answers on the aspects of writing which are covered in the actual test. These aspects of writing are called 'assessment focuses'. The chart on page 130 explains the assessment focuses for each writing task.

The longer task

● How you structure and punctuate sentences. For example:
  – Do you use a variety of simple, compound and complex sentences to clarify your meaning?
  – Are your sentences grammatically correct and accurately punctuated?
  – Are you able to use a range of punctuation, such as semi-colons, direct speech and dashes?
	8 marks

● How you organise paragraphs and ensure that your writing 'hangs together' well. For example:
  – Do you use main or topic sentences in paragraphs to help your readers follow the sense of your writing?
  – Do you group and link paragraphs on a similar theme?
  – Do you use connecting words and phrases that show how your ideas are developing?
	8 marks

● The overall impact of your writing on the reader. For example:
  – Have you written with purpose and audience clearly in mind?
  – Have you established and maintained a clear and consistent point of view?
  – Has your choice of language and technical devices, such as imagery, enhanced the effect of your writing?
	14 marks

The shorter task

● How you structure, punctuate and organise sentences. For example: how accurately do you construct and vary sentences for clarity, purpose and effect?	*6 marks*
● The overall impact of your writing on the reader. For example: do you write appropriately for the purpose and audience?	*10 marks*
● The accuracy of your spelling. For example: do you spell correctly a range of simple and more challenging words?	*4 marks*

Express yourself well

Here are a few tips for writing good responses.

- Take time to **plan your response**. Read each task carefully, make notes and plan what you are going to write. Before you start writing, check that your plan responds to the actual task and that you are not going to write about things which are not relevant.
- Use as many of the **skills** that you have learned and that are appropriate to the question as you can, for example in your choice of persuasive or descriptive language.
- Watch your **spelling** and **punctuation**.
- Make sure what you have written **makes sense**. If you realise it does not, change it. If you cannot understand what you have written, it is unlikely the marker will!
- Try to leave a few minutes at the end to **check your response** carefully.
- Think about your **handwriting** even if you are in a hurry. After all, you cannot score marks if the marker cannot read what you have written!

Using the practice tests

The practice writing tests in this book are similar to the actual test (except for the planning frames which are provided here for the shorter writing tasks but are not provided in the actual test). If you attempt these tasks during Year 9, the results will show you and your teacher where you have improved your writing skills since Year 8. The results will also highlight areas of your writing that might still be improved before you take the test. You can then go back through this book and revise the skills and strategies you need.

When you receive the results of the Key Stage 3 tests, the marks for both writing tasks will be combined to give you an overall National Curriculum level for writing. You will also receive a separate National Curriculum level for reading, and a combined reading and writing level for English. This will show you exactly what your strengths and weaknesses are, and will allow you to focus on areas that will improve your writing beyond Key Stage 3.

Good luck!

Longer writing task 1:
Writing to imagine, explore, entertain

You should spend about 45 minutes on this task, including 15 minutes' planning time.

The beginning ...
You have seen the following notice in a local newspaper and decide to enter the competition.

To all young writers!

Are you a Year 9 pupil attending a school in Newtown?

Do you enjoy writing prose fiction?

Would you like to win a prize for yourself and your school?

If your answer is 'yes', read on!

The Editor of the Newtown Chronicle announces a competition to find the best opening to a novel or short story written by a Year 9 pupil in a Newtown school.

Remember – it is just the opening: I need to see if you can capture my interest!

Send your entry by the given date and you could win £50 for yourself and £200 of books for your school library.

Write your entry for the competition. It should be the opening 300–350 words of a novel or short story.

Remember to:
- keep to the requirement for an **opening** only
- write in an appropriate style which will interest your readers
- use the planning frame to help you organise your ideas.

30 marks

The beginning ...

Use a planning grid like the one below to help you to plan your work. (This page will not be marked.)

Type or genre of story

Some typical features of this type or genre

Setting	Descriptive words / phrases

Characters	Appearance / actions / words

Ideas for opening sentence(s)

Longer writing task 2:
Writing to inform, explain, describe

You should spend about 45 minutes on this task, including 15 minutes' planning time.

Advice to a new School Council representative

The school year is almost over and your term of office as a Year 9 representative on the School Council is almost over.

The notice below, calling for the new form representatives, has been posted on the class noticeboard.

Newtown Community High School

Elections to the School Council

These elections will be held at the end of next week. If you would like to be your form's representative on the School Council next year, you should give your name to your form tutor. Your tutor will explain the election process to you this week.

Form representatives should be prepared to:

- listen to the views and ideas of members of their form
- attend all meetings of the School Council
- take part in decision making
- report decisions back to their form
- represent the school at functions such as parents' evenings.

You have been asked to write a briefing note for pupils who are considering standing for election to the School Council for next year. These pupils, who have not been on a School Council before, need to know what their duties will involve. You could also give some advice about the pleasures and pressures of the post.

Write the briefing note for Year 9 representatives on the School Council. It should be about 300–350 words long.

Remember to:
- write in a style which is appropriate to secondary school pupils
- bring your advice to life with examples of what you have had to do
- use the planning frame to help you organise your ideas.

30 marks

Advice to a new School Council representative

Use a planning grid like the one below to help you to plan your work. (This page will not be marked.)

Welcoming opening

Official duties	Comments / examples

Pleasures	Pressures

Encouraging ending

Longer writing task 3:
Writing to persuade, argue, advise

You should spend about 45 minutes on this task, including 15 minutes' planning time.

Applying for a grant

You are the chairperson of your local youth club committee. You have received the following information about new grants which are available.

NEWTOWN COUNCIL

Notice of grants to youth organisations

We wish to fund improvements in our provision for young people in the Newtown area. One way will be through allocating money to existing youth organisations.

You may apply for a grant if you hold a position of authority in a youth organisation. You should submit a report to me, at the Town Hall, which details:

- the facilities already available to your members and how these facilities could be improved
- additional needs of young people in your area for which there is currently no provision
- reasons why funding your organisation should be a priority for the Newtown Town Council.

Harold Smith, Clerk to the Town Council

Write the report, which should be about 300–350 words long.

Remember to:
- follow the guidance in the notice above
- write in an appropriately formal style
- use the planning frame to help you organise your ideas.

30 marks

Applying for a grant

Use a planning grid like the one below to help you to plan your work. (This page will not be marked.)

Facilities to be improved	Additional facilities needed

Reasons why this youth club should be given funding

Ideas for opening	Ideas for ending

Reminders about writing formally

Longer writing task 4:
Writing to analyse, review, comment

You should spend about 45 minutes on this task, including 15 minutes' planning time.

In the news

Your local radio station broadcasts a weekly current affairs programme for young people. In this programme, they provide opportunities for listeners to comment on news items that interest them.

The radio station provides the following guidelines for potential speakers.

Radio Newtown

`Voicebox`
Guidelines for broadcasters

Please send us your proposed script, following this advice:

1 Prepare your material thoroughly – check your facts and sources.

2 Explain the background to the story – not everyone will know as much as you.

3 Remember that will be speaking to a teenage audience.

4 When you are giving your own views, make this clear – comment on other people's views as well where you can.

Above all, respect your listeners and treat them with courtesy.

Your script should be about 300–350 words in length.

Think of a recent news item that has captured your interest. It might be local, national or international.

Write the proposed script for your broadcast.

Remember to:
- follow the radio station's guidelines
- use the planning frame to help you organise your ideas.

30 marks

In the news

Use a planning grid like the one below to help you to plan your work. (This page will not be marked.)

Topic chosen	Why it interests me

Main features of news item

My own views

What others have said about it	What I feel about their views

Ideas for a strong opening statement	Ideas for a memorable closing statement

Shorter writing task 1
(Writing to imagine, explore, entertain)
You should spend 30 minutes on this task.

Fortune tellers required

Some people use fortune tellers to help them make decisions and to plan their personal lives and careers.

Here is an extract from an advertisement that has appeared in a newspaper.

Fortune tellers required!

This is your opportunity to join the League of Fortune Tellers (LOFT) and play your part in shaping people's lives.

Write to the address below, giving evidence of your ability to foretell the future and saying what you could contribute to the League.

Write your reply to the advertisement, in no more than 200 words.

Remember to think carefully about:
- what you choose to include in your reply;
- the style of writing you use to interest your readers.

The planning frame will help you organise your ideas before you start to write.

20 marks including 4 marks for spelling

Fortune tellers required!

Use a planning grid like the one below to help you to plan your writing.

Ideas for a catchy opening to my reply

What are my special qualities or powers as a fortune teller?

What amazing things have I done with these powers in the past?

Why would they be valuable to people?

How can I end my reply in a way that leaves the reader interested?

Shorter writing task 2
(Writing to inform, explain, describe)
You should spend 30 minutes on this task.

Everything You Need to Know!

This is a note from your Head Teacher.

Dear Year 9 student

As you know, we are preparing a booklet for new Year 7 students called 'Everything You Need to Know' which tells them all about our school and its facilities. We still need someone to write the section on extra activities, clubs and sports. Are you that person?

This is your chance to pass on what you know. We want to provide a clear picture of what is on offer so that the new Year 7s will feel welcome and will want to join in.

I'm really looking forward to seeing what you have to say!

Joyce Williams

Head Teacher

Write the section about extra activities, clubs and sports for the Year 7 booklet, in no more than 200 words.

Remember to think carefully about:
- what you choose to include in your reply;
- the style of writing you use to interest your readers.

The planning frame will help you organise your ideas before you start to write.

20 marks including 4 marks for spelling

Everything You Need to Know!

Use a planning grid like the one below to help you to plan your writing.

Ideas for an interesting opening

Extra activities

Clubs

Sports

Ideas for a memorable ending

Shorter writing task 3
(Writing to persuade, argue, advise)
You should spend 30 minutes on this task.

A charity event

Your school is organising a charity 'Sports and Fun Day' and would like to invite a famous person to open it.

Write a letter to a famous person of your choice – it might be a TV or sports personality – to persuade them to open your charity day.

Remember to think carefully about how you will persuade the famous person.

Write the letter, in no more than 200 words

The planning frame will help you organise your ideas before you start to write.

20 marks including 4 marks for spelling

A charity event

Use a planning grid like the one below to help you plan your writing.

Ideas for a memorable opening to the letter

Information about the charity event

Reasons why the famous person might want to open this charity event

---

Words and phrases to persuade

Ideas for a memorable ending to the letter

Shorter writing task 4
(Writing to analyse, review, comment)

You should spend 30 minutes on this task.

Computer games and you

You read the following advertisement in a teenage magazine:

We're planning an article in next month's magazine about young people and computer games and we want to include your comments.

- How often do you play computer games?

- Why do you play computer games?

- Do you think it's a good use of your time?

- Are computer games stopping you from doing other things?

Write and tell us what you think.

Write your views for the teenage magazine, in no more than 200 words.

Remember to:
- answer all the questions in your reply;
- give reasons for your views;
- think carefully about the best way to get your ideas across.

The planning frame will help you organise your ideas before you start to write.

20 marks including 4 marks for spelling

Computer games and you

Use a planning grid like the one below to help you plan your writing.

> **How often do I play computer games?**

> **Why do I play computer games?**

> **Is it a good use of my time?**

> **Are computer games stopping me from doing other things?**

> **Words / phrases to introduce my ideas / opinions**

F Skills bank

This section focuses on some essential writing skills that you can use in all the writing you do. The activities will help you to make progress with your writing skills and support you when you do the writing tasks in the rest of the book.
You can use the activities in two different ways:

- to remind yourself of a particular skill before you start writing

- to check your work against the information given in this section after you have finished writing.

↘ Writing in complete sentences

ACTIVITY 1

Look at the groups of words below. Only five of them are complete sentences. Decide which are complete sentences and write them out, using full stops and capital letters. If you have selected the correct sentences, you will see that they can be linked together.

a   in period 1 the Physics teacher was in a grumpy mood all lesson
b   as cold as ice
c   while watching my dad change the car tyre
d   the school bus turned up very late
e   lovely colours in the sky
f   it was a bad day for Jonathan from the start
g   on a crowded beach with many water sport attractions
h   he had forgotten to bring in his PE kit for period 2
i   a rather scruffy boy with bright blue eyes
j   instead of playing football he had to read a boring book in the library

 REMEMBER

A sentence is a group of words that makes sense on its own. It starts with a capital letter and ends with a full stop or the equivalent punctuation.

Linking sentences into paragraphs

1 Write down the five sentences you selected in Activity 1 in the correct order so that they tell part of a story. This now makes one complete paragraph and is the beginning of a story about Jonathan's bad day at school.

2 Now think about how you would continue the story. For example, you might want to mention what happened between the PE lesson and lunchtime.

3 Decide which of the following groups of words would give the best start to the second paragraph of this story:

a After leaving the library …
b Going to the music room …
c Mr Jenkins was approaching like a …
d At break in the dining room …
e Standing in the library corridor … .

4 Write five or six groups of words on your ideas about what should go into the second paragraph of the story.

5 Now write five or six complete sentences, with full stops and capital letters, to make the second paragraph in the story of Jonathan's bad day.

 REMEMBER

The first words of each new paragraph are very important. They need to have a clear link to the paragraph before. By including clear links like this you will give your writing a successful structure, built up paragraph by paragraph.

Using topic sentences to improve paragraph organisation

In some forms of writing, you may be asked to give some information, possibly as part of an argument or an explanation, or to persuade or advise your readers. It is helpful to open each paragraph with a sentence clearly telling readers what will be in that paragraph.

1 Look at these examples of three different topic sentences.

> Now I will tell you where reggae music came from.

> There are two Premier League football teams in Liverpool.

> In the Canary Islands, Lanzarote is a popular holiday destination.

2 Using each of these sentences as the opening topic sentence, write the paragraph that follows. (You may have to do some research in the library, on the Internet or at home for this.) Remember to write in complete sentences with capital letters and full stops.

↘ Using adverbs and adjectives

Adverbs

Using adverbs well makes your meaning perfectly clear and allows you to be more precise in your writing. Look at how this can work in real examples.

> I want you to tidy up your bedroom.

This is a rather general instruction – you could set about this attractive task at any time! But in the following sentence, the addition of the adverb 'instantly' gives a much clearer meaning to the instruction.

> I want you to tidy up your bedroom instantly.

Notice also how adding the adverb can affect the tone of the writing. In the first sentence the tone is quite vague. Try saying it in different voices. It could be rather desperate and pleading. However, in the second sentence the tone is clearer. It is forceful and demanding. All this has been achieved by adding one adverb to a simple sentence.

Adjectives

Using adjectives can have a similar impact on your writing as using adverbs. Look at the following example.

> The house stood at the end of a lane.

We can get a picture in our minds from this description, but it is vague. Houses come in a variety of styles, and lanes can be long, short, wide or narrow. Look at the effect created by adding adjectives to the sentence. The image is now much clearer and more precise.

Gives an impression of the size of the house.

Suggests the time of year and helps create an image of light, shade and movement.

> The looming, deserted house stood at the end of a leafy lane.

Gives a picture of the house looking empty, maybe even starting to decay.

Notice how the adjectives also affect the tone. The scene now seems rather spooky, with a threatening tone. A ghostly atmosphere is also being built up. All this has been achieved by adding a few adjectives to a simple sentence.

You have seen how the use of adjectives and adverbs can contribute to meaning and tone, but they need to be chosen carefully to achieve the right effect – they shouldn't be overdone or underdone.

ACTIVITY 4

1   Look at this example in which the writer has depended on a limited choice of adjectives.

> The holiday got off to a good start. We had a nice journey on the plane and arrived on time. Our hotel room looked pretty and there was a good range of facilities available in the hotel. The beach looked nice in the sunshine. The sea was warm and the nice smell from the small cafés on the waterfront added to a good feeling about the place.

The writer has tried to use adjectives, but they are not very precise and they are rather repetitive.

2   Work with a partner. Discuss what atmosphere the writer was trying to create in this description of a holiday resort.
3   Re-write the description using more precise adjectives to create the atmosphere you have decided on.

ACTIVITY 5

1   Now look at another piece of writing. The writer is trying to create a feeling of escape from danger, but the atmosphere of fear and desperation isn't very strong.

> Bill walked down the road. He was looking for somewhere to hide. The gang was approaching and he needed to get under cover. Finally, he spotted a small gap in the fence, which led into some thick woodland.

2   Add four adverbs that will make the writer's intention clearer and more precise.

↘ Sentence punctuation

Punctuation at the end of sentences is the most straightforward. On page 148 you have already looked at what makes a sentence and you know that most sentences end with a full stop. For example:

I almost missed the school bus this morning.

However, if that sentence is turned into a question, the punctuation changes from a full stop (.) to a question mark (?). For example:

Did you catch the school bus this morning?

Another way to punctuate the end of sentences is with an exclamation mark. This is used at the end of command sentences, which are also called imperatives. For example:

Pick up your clothes from the floor!

Sometimes just single word imperatives are used. For example:

Stop!   March!

Exclamation marks can also be used to emphasise the feeling expressed in a sentence.

What a boring evening that was!

ACTIVITY 6

Add the correct punctuation to the end of these sentences.
a   Was the weather fine at the coast
b   Eat your vegetables now
c   The town closed early today
d   Go
e   Who has taken my pencils
f   That story in assembly was so inspiring
g   The holidays are all booked up
h   Has it been such a struggle to do the shopping

↘ Using commas in a sentence

Commas are used to separate parts of a sentence. For example, commas are used to mark off extra information:

> The local football team tried hard today but the opposition, helped by the referee, won in the end.

Commas can be used after a subodinate clause which begins a sentence. For example:

> Because it was his birthday, I lent him my skateboard.

They can also be used to separate items in a list to avoid using 'and' repetitively. For example:

> After a long, tiring day we arrived home dishevelled, footsore, tired and extremely hungry.

This example has used a list of adjectives, but the same rule applies to a list of nouns, verbs or adverbs.

ACTIVITY 7

Add the correct punctuation to the end of each of these sentences and add commas correctly within them.

a   Did I see the parents teachers caretakers and some pupils helping to clean up the mess

b   Nigel my dog sleeps in the conservatory

c   Slowly carefully and vigilantly the tiger stalked its tired vulnerable prey

d   What a hopeless unfit and incompetent lot we are

e   Although I asked her nicely my sister wouldn't lend me £50

f   After a hopeless search we found nothing but old bottles despite information from Grandad

Apostrophes

To indicate possession

There is sometimes confusion over where to place apostrophes, but we do need them to make meanings clear. For example:

> the boys books

Without the apostrophe, it is unclear whether we are talking about one boy or more than one boy. The use of the apostrophe makes this clear – before the 's' for the singular, i.e. one boy ...

> the boy's books

... or after the 's' for the plural, i.e. more than one boy.

> the boys' books

If a word already ends in 's', we simply place the apostrophe after the final 's'. For example:

> St James' Park   Sibelius' symphony

Some plural words do not end in an 's'. For example:

> children   women

Here we put the apostrophe before the 's', i.e. after the plural form. For example:

> children's   women's

To indicate missing letters

The other use of the apostrophe is to indicate where letters are missing in some words. This happens particularly in more informal styles of writing. In this case, the apostrophe goes where the letter or letters have been missed out. For example:

> did not ⟶ didn't
> cannot ⟶ can't
> of the clock ⟶ o'clock

Remember that 'it's', i.e. with an apostrophe, can only mean 'it is'.

ACTIVITY 8

Place apostrophes where needed in these sentences.
a   I couldnt find the childrens PE kit anywhere.
b   The butchers dog cheerfully wagged its tail.
c   The teachers staffroom was locked but the heads office was open.
d   Dont eat your lunch in a hurry.
e   Its always busy on the towns ring road in the evening.

Phrases and clauses

You already know that a sentence is a group of words which makes sense on its own. You also know how to indicate the end of a sentence correctly, with a full stop. For example:

> The teacher started the lesson promptly.

Phrases

However, the sentence above is a very simple one. To make your sentences more interesting, you can make them longer and more complex. For example, the teacher could be more interesting:

> The teacher, grumpy and impatient, started the lesson promptly.

The group of words 'grumpy and impatient' come as a group after the word 'teacher', rather than as single adjectives before it. A group of words like this, which makes sense within the sentence but cannot stand alone, is called a **phrase**. Because it is being used to describe the teacher, it is an adjectival phrase.

We could say more about when the lesson started. For example:

> The teacher started the lesson at the correct time.

Here, the phrase 'at the correct time' replaces the adverb 'promptly'; it is an adverbial phrase.

We could also have introduced the teacher in a slightly different way:

> Mr Douglas, the Geography teacher, started the lesson promptly.

Here, the phrase 'the Geography teacher' is part of the naming of Mr Douglas; it is a noun phrase.

Clauses

We could have varied the sentence in another way. For example:

> Mr Douglas, who teaches Geography at our school, started the lesson promptly.

The group of words 'who teaches Geography' makes the sentence more complex, as does a phrase, but it includes a verb. A group of words like this, formed around a verb, is called a **clause**. By using clauses and thinking about where you put them in a sentence, you can make your writing more varied and effective.

ACTIVITY 9

Combine the following pieces of information into complex sentences using phrases and clauses.

a   busy street; you live there; traffic calming measures; local council policy.

b   holiday resort; lively and bustling; attractive to teenagers.

c   school homework; place to do it; idea of head teacher; school library; after school.

↘ Direct speech

Using direct speech in a piece of writing can have considerable advantages. It can make the writing very realistic. It can add to the readers' impression of a character because they can read the character's actual words. It's a way of introducing informal and colloquial language into your writing, which can make it lively and interesting.

However, it is important to show where the speech starts and finishes so that your readers can see who is saying what, and where their words start and finish.

Start by putting the inverted commas, or speech marks, around the words actually spoken. For example:

> Tom said, 'Put all the footballs in the skip!'

Take note of:

- the position of the speech marks – the speaker's words are all placed inside the speech marks
- the first word actually spoken, 'Put', has a capital letter even though it is not the first word in the sentence or a proper noun
- the words actually spoken are split off from the rest of the sentence with a comma
- the final punctuation, in this case an exclamation mark, comes inside the final speech mark.

You may want to have more than one character speaking. Remember that every time a different character starts to speak, you must start a new paragraph.

> 'I can't find my new CD,' Mary wailed to her mother.
> 'If you looked after your music,' her mother replied, 'then I wouldn't have to tidy it up for you.'

Notice that in the sentence above the speaker's words fall into two parts. A comma is used after 'music' to show that the sentence continues, and the second part does not need a capital letter.

ACTIVITY 10

Now put the speech marks into these pieces of writing, starting a new paragraph where necessary.

> Ted's camping weekend had not got off to a good start. I can't find my sleeping bag he cried after school on Friday. You could look on top of your wardrobe his mother replied. Do you think it might be there? Ted asked. I'm sure I saw it yesterday said his mother while I was chasing the cat.

> The patient was not happy. When can I see a doctor he begged the nurse. When one is free the nurse replied, giving him a cold stare. After he had looked at the other patients all he could say was Thank heaven I'm not as ill as some of them.

Acknowledgements

The publishers gratefully acknowledge the following for permission to reproduce copyright material. Every effort has been made to contact copyright holders of material reproduced in this book. Any omissions will be rectified in subsequent printings if notice is given to the publishers.

Extract from *Innocent Blood* by P. D. James, published by Faber and Faber Limited. Reprinted with permission of the publishers Faber and Faber Limited. Extract from *Have The Men Had Enough?* By Margaret Forster, published by Chatto & Windus. Used by permission of The Random House Group Limited. Extracts from *Questions in El Salvidor* by David Brierly, *Five Days in Guinea* by Andrew Dinwoodie, *Boys' own expedition* by Nick Kirke and *Midnight on Mont Blanc* by R. G. Willis, all taken from *The Best of Sunday Times Travel* published by David & Charles, 1998. Reprinted by kind permission of the publishers. Extract from *Crow Road* by Iain Banks published by Abacus Books. Reprinted with permission of Time Warner Books UK. Extract from *Face* by Benjamin Zephaniah, published by Bloomsbury. Reprinted with permission of Bloomsbury. Extracts from *Northern Lights* by Philip Pullman. Copyright © Philip Pullman, 1995, the first volume of the HIS DARK MATERIALS trilogy, published by Scholastic Children's Books. All rights reserved. Reproduced by permission of Scholastic Limited. Extract from *Terra Incognita* by Sarah Wheeler, published by Jonathan Cape. Used by permission of The Random House Group Limited. Extract from *Pygmalion* by George Bernard Shaw. Reprinted by permission of The Society of Authors on behalf of the Bernard Shaw Estate. Extract red nose day. Reprinted by permission of Comic Relief UK. Extract from *Like Water For Chocolate* by Laura Esquival published by Black Swan. Copyright © Seventh Dimension Entertainment Co. Inc 1993. Used by permission of Transworld Publishers, a division of The Random House Group Limited. Extract from *Perfume: The Story of a Murder* by Patrick Suskind (Hamish Hamilton 1985) Copyright © Patrick Suskind, 1985. Reprinted with permission of Penguin Books UK. Extract from *The Spirit of St. Louis* by Charles Lindbergh, published by John Murray (Publishers) Limited. Reprinted by permission of the publishers. 'Green Iguana Care' written by Dr. Jenni Bass and Edited by Dr Nancy Anderson, take from www.petplace.com . Reprinted with permission of Intelligent Content Corporation, USA. Extract from *Keeping Your Tarantula Healthy: A Quick Guide* by Fred Sherberger. Extracts of text from www.feathers.co.uk. Reprinted with the kind permission of The Feathers Hotel, Oxford. Extract from www.switchmagazine.com. Reprinted with the kind permission of Switch Magazine. Extract 'What does a veterinary nurse do? From BBC CBBC Online www.bbc.co.uk/cbbc/wild/working/nurse.shtml. Reprinted by permission of the BBC. Extract from www.appcpenn.org. Reprinted by permission of The Annenberg Public Policy Center, University of Pennsylvania. Extract from *The Book of Dolphins* by Mark Carwardine, published by Dragon's World, 1996. Copyright © Mark Carwardine. Reprinted with the kind permission of the author. Extract on St. Petersburg. Reprinted with the kind permission of Pilot Productions. Extract from *Ten Arms and a Giant's Eye* by Lee Krystek. Reprinted with the kind permission of the author. Extract from *Ordinary Seaman* by John Gordon published by Walker Books. Copyright © John Gordon, 1992. Reprinted with permission of the publishers. Extract from *Among The Russians* by Colin Thubron, published by Heinemann. Used by permission of The Random House Group Limited. 'Fatal delays that trapped crowds' by Ed Vuillimay, The Guardian 13th September, 2001. Copyright © The Guardian. Used with permission. Extract from 'Vandalism threatens future of skate park', The Oxford Times, 25th July, 2003. Reprinted with the kind permission of editorial at The Oxford Times. extract from seventeen.com. Extract from *The Truth About Mount Kinabalu* by Dr. Jocasta Webb. Reprinted with the kind permission of the author. Review of 'Dinomania: Things to do with Dinosaurs' by Mick Manning and Brita Granstrom, published by Watts. Review by Lindsey Fraser. Reprinted with the kind permission of Lindsey Fraser & Guardian newspapers. Review of 'Lord of the Rings' *Precious Metal* written by Tim Curphey. Reprinted with the kind permission of Tim Curphey. 'Why hip hop must take its share of the Blame' by Caroline Sullivan, The Guardian, 6th January, 2003. Copyright © Caroline Sullivan, 2003. Used with permission. Quotes by Ivor Etienne, Elaine Sihera and Lucy Cope, from The Observer, 5th January 2003. Used with permission. 'Respecting rap' The Guardian, 8th January, 2003. Copyright © The Guardian. Used with permission.